T0135003

Human–Computer Interaction Series

Editors-in-Chief

Desney Tan
Microsoft Research, Redmond, WA, USA

Jean Vanderdonckt
Louvain School of Management, Université catholique de Louvain,
Louvain-La-Neuve, Belgium

The Human–Computer Interaction Series, launched in 2004, publishes books that advance the science and technology of developing systems which are effective and satisfying for people in a wide variety of contexts. Titles focus on theoretical perspectives (such as formal approaches drawn from a variety of behavioural sciences), practical approaches (such as techniques for effectively integrating user needs in system development), and social issues (such as the determinants of utility, usability and acceptability).

HCI is a multidisciplinary field and focuses on the human aspects in the development of computer technology. As technology becomes increasingly more pervasive the need to take a human-centred approach in the design and development of computer-based systems becomes ever more important.

Titles published within the Human–Computer Interaction Series are included in Thomson Reuters' Book Citation Index, The DBLP Computer Science Bibliography and The HCI Bibliography.

More information about this series at http://www.springer.com/series/6033

Kei Hoshi · John Waterworth

Primitive Interaction Design

Springer

Kei Hoshi
Auckland, New Zealand

John Waterworth
Umeå, Västerbottens Län, Sweden

ISSN 1571-5035 ISSN 2524-4477 (electronic)
Human–Computer Interaction Series
ISBN 978-3-030-42956-0 ISBN 978-3-030-42954-6 (eBook)
https://doi.org/10.1007/978-3-030-42954-6

© Springer Nature Switzerland AG 2020
This work is subject to copyright. All rights are reserved by the Publisher, whether the whole or part of the material is concerned, specifically the rights of translation, reprinting, reuse of illustrations, recitation, broadcasting, reproduction on microfilms or in any other physical way, and transmission or information storage and retrieval, electronic adaptation, computer software, or by similar or dissimilar methodology now known or hereafter developed.
The use of general descriptive names, registered names, trademarks, service marks, etc. in this publication does not imply, even in the absence of a specific statement, that such names are exempt from the relevant protective laws and regulations and therefore free for general use.
The publisher, the authors and the editors are safe to assume that the advice and information in this book are believed to be true and accurate at the date of publication. Neither the publisher nor the authors or the editors give a warranty, expressed or implied, with respect to the material contained herein or for any errors or omissions that may have been made. The publisher remains neutral with regard to jurisdictional claims in published maps and institutional affiliations.

This Springer imprint is published by the registered company Springer Nature Switzerland AG
The registered company address is: Gewerbestrasse 11, 6330 Cham, Switzerland

The first author dedicates this book to all those who go along the middle of the road, who are seen on the left when viewed from the right, and on the right when viewed from the left. Walk with your head held high on the road.

The second author dedicates this book to all those who appreciate the beauty of a freshly ploughed field.

Preface

This book has its origins in issues raised by our earlier text *Human-Experiential Design of Presence in Everyday Blended Reality: Living in the Here and Now* (Waterworth and Hoshi 2016). In that first book, we explored the possibilities for designing "blended spaces" to overcome the fragmented sense of psychological presence we all feel in the mixed digital and physical realities we inhabit. We presented a first version of what we called "Human-Experiential Design", a theme we take up in more detail here. In the course of motivating that approach to design, we touched on certain untapped sources for design insights, including a consideration of myth, and the importance of the unconscious.

In the present book, we expand and develop these and other insights into a more fully fledged approach to interaction design. We are motivated by the belief that—despite or, to some extent, because of—the influential role design plays in the creation and marketing of interactive artefacts, interaction design has lost its way. We need to step back and open up to the changes that technology has brought to our lives, not all of them beneficial, and to open up to fundamental aspects of the human condition. Primitive interaction design attempts to do both and suggests a way forward.

Recently, designers have had serious doubts about their own job, the responsibility of a designer. Even if they fulfil the responsibility with the best intentions to make good products that improve daily life, they are in a way just glamourizing the ownership of things. It is maybe a romantic and nostalgic idea to imagine that designing for the essential true nature of our aesthetic life can survive recent rapid commercial development of our globe, what people are calling *globalism*. Designers have the responsibility to ensure that human beings remain in the world of things, so people will buy and use things for better reasons than simply to possess them.

Contemporary society produces and consumes in vast quantities. We then discard vast amounts of garbage. Our apprehension about the amount perhaps needs to be displaced with apprehension about the speed of consumption. Everyone thinks that production has no meaning without speed. We panic because of unseen competitors. The speed of our creation of amounts of products has the immediacy to shock and surprise especially when we encounter and recognize aesthetic value as well.

People should no longer have to tolerate the pain that much current design of technology brings. The quest for speed in our contemporary society continues to destroy the environment, as well as a measured and reflective way of living. Perhaps speed is not our inevitable evolution but only a reflection of recent rapid changes in our society. Although we think that we really should slow down, that would be difficult to accomplish. That is because of the fear of doing something akin to stopping in the path of a rush-hour crowd. People have certainly taken speed to be a value, and in the flow of time we can no longer experience the benefits and pleasures of living that had been part of our former way of life, which the older generation probably enjoyed to a greater extent. Essentially, slow is the true nature of our aesthetic life, and perhaps especially for the vulnerable, the elderly and the socially handicapped, who have become increasingly marginalized with increases in the speed of change of our society. But industries cannot slow down their production. Designers optimistically think that simple shapes create a simple society.

In our current reckless industrial era, the market desires strong impressions of owning products—sometimes visually, sometimes functionally. The market becomes timid in the face of design that does not draw customers' consciousness, because design should be a tool to encourage customers to buy. There is a fundamental marketing assumption that design draws customers' consciousnesses with attractive products and interfaces. Yet, this same consciousness breaks the human's natural flow of action, sometimes perceptually, sometimes physically.

It should not be the case that we are aware, in the here and now, and then pick up a product and act. This is generally quite unnatural and implies explicit knowledge and conscious effort. Rather, when functioning smoothly, we act without conscious awareness and then find later that we have been using a tool (usually when something goes wrong). Tangible interaction, unconsciously executed and informed by peripheral information, restores the primacy of action and re-integrates the mind and the body. The technology then disappears from perception in use. That means that products/artefacts have to be designed for human beings, not users or customers.

People end up grabbing a handrail for balance or warming hands on a hot mug without any conscious thought. There is no conscious effort in the behaviours, because the experience that has already made possible the series of actions, but unconsciously. It is the implicit memory that our bodies know, rather than the explicit and abstract knowledge that we are conscious of and can talk about. The designer needs not to create a body warmer that draws consciousness, but a hot mug becomes a body warmer without thought, because it already exists in our unconscious memory.

Everyone says that design should be simple and inconspicuous, so that people are not aware of the design. But design is actually inseparable from the background environment composed of everything that exists around the design, such as human experiences and memories; customs and behaviours; history and culture; technology and trends; time and circumstance; and atmosphere, sound/noise and air. If one of the elements even slightly changes, the design impression changes too. Human beings share the whole. These days, many people in industry and academia say that they want to design products/artefacts that touch peoples' heartstrings. But if it is about drawing out human consciousness, we would say: please don't touch our hearts (our consciousness) so easily. To be pleasant and invigorating, human life should be free of the need to always be conscious of the environment in which it exists. We should be like the fish coming free into a clear stream from a mudflow, by struggling to swim.

Society has become more savage and less cultured, despite—or because of—the interactive devices that permeate our lives. In this book, we try to shed light on how our thinking of design and information-based society should adapt by using more a more universal approach and aspects of human consciousness/unconsciousness in a new, "primitive" coexistence with modern information technology.

Auckland, New Zealand — Kei Hoshi
Umeå, Sweden — John Waterworth

Contents

Part II Theories and Foundations

Part III Design Untamed

List of Figures

Part I
Motivations and Inspirations

In Part I, we outline motivating arguments for change in the way interaction design is conceived and carried out. We start by questioning recent views of the designer's role and of modern information society, stressing that design should not merely be a menial servant to the economical world. We are inspired by an alternative way of looking at interaction design, Human-Experiential Design (HXD) that we introduced in a previous volume (Waterworth and Hoshi, 2016) and that represents a starting point for a different approach to "human-centred design". It also provides a reframed categorization of customer, user, person and human, which allows us to discover new aspects of the human and inspires a richer view of what human-centredness means.

We then propose a new direction for interaction design grounded in mythical thought and an understanding of the "savage" stage of being (being without language; Lévi-Strauss, 1966), which helps us pursue more intimately the nature of being and beings, adopting a circular historical view of human progress closer to eastern philosophy than western determinism. A key point, often lost in contemporary societal role ascription, is that we all share the reality that we are human and living on Earth, and all that entails in terms of experience and understanding. From our perspective, this is the most valuable design resource we have, although it is barely recognized by current conceptions of what interaction design is, who does it, and for whom it is done.

Chapter 1
Why Primitive Interaction Design?

It is wholly indeterminate. It has no specific traits. It is entirely ineffable. It is never seen. It is not accessible.
Barry, Robert (1970). It is wholly indeterminate. Graphic installation work.

Abstract In the first section of this first chapter, we consider how interaction design came to be the way it is, by selectively reviewing the relevant context from the history of design and of human–computer interaction (HCI). This motivates the need for a new approach to interaction design. In the second section, we outline the inspirations and background for we call Primitive Interaction Design, which leads us into the remainder of the book.

1.1 Introduction

Today, we live in a world into which electronic technologies have penetrated pervasively, in a market-driven society where everyday reality consists, to an extent, in consuming the fruits of technological development. In this situation, designers discharge their duties supported by arguments from instrumental rationality, with flare and some imagination, but largely under the spell of practical reasoning. This book is founded on the belief that designers need to be free from the marketplace and industry pressure so as to have the possibility to explore other ideas and issues, and this book offers a way to address this need without falling back on the usual user-centred arguments from interaction design research. In fact, we see part of the problem as residing in the conception of the people for whom these products are designed as "users" or, even worse, as "consumers". Even though they are of course users and consumers, the design of more humane—and interesting—interactive products requires that they be seen as fully human beings, and that the designer too is also fully human and much more than an instrumentally rational practical reasoner, however successful an individual designer may be in market terms.

© Springer Nature Switzerland AG 2020

K. Hoshi and J. Waterworth, *Primitive Interaction Design*,
Human–Computer Interaction Series,
https://doi.org/10.1007/978-3-030-42954-6_1

Interaction design is currently seen as an important area of study, and more especially of design practice. Hugely popular and profitable consumer devices, in particular, mobile phones and tablet PCs, are recognized as owing much of their success to the way they have been designed, not least their interface characteristics and the styles of interaction that they support. Interaction design studies point to the importance of a user-centred approach, whereby products are designed around their future users' needs and capacities, and so enhance their capabilities and lives. However, interaction design as a practical occupation is not closely aligned with interaction design as an area of academic study, and design theorists have speculated for some time on the extent to which research studies in interaction design actually influence the way products are designed in practice, and how this can be maximized. Be that as it may, it is the market, and marketing, that determines what products are available for people to interact with and, to some extent, how they interact.

In the first section of this chapter, we consider how interaction design came to be the way it is, by selectively reviewing the context from the history of design and of human–computer interaction (HCI), which motivates the need for a new approach to interaction design. In the second section, we outline the inspirations and background for we call Primitive Interaction Design, which leads us into the remainder of the book.

1.2 Interaction Design in Context

What is interaction design? In addressing this question, we have to step back and consider design itself. Design has been discussed as crafts work by a large number of recent scholars, including several from the field of HCI (e.g. Long and Dowell 1989; Rosner 2009; Fetaji et al. 2007; Plass 1998; Chalmers 1996; Benyon 2002; Wright et al. 2006; Norman 2007). They frequently describe designing as an activity of craftsmanship that deals with internal images and subjective sense, it also contains aspects that are hard to illustrate through theoretical points of view. They use such terms as "tacit", "experiential", "unknowable", "skilled physical manipulation by hands" and so on as main elements of crafts. However, it is doubtful whether many design professions recognize themselves as craftsmen.

1.3 Subjective Versus Objective Views

Looking into the details of well-designed things, we realize the amazingly rich thought process that is condensed in them. We see that there are logical decisions in the detail of making things incorporate subjective senses. Designers synthesize various conditions such as functionalities, use scenarios and material characteristics as if they were weaving those conditions into fabrics in which their design is realized. Well-designed things are a depiction of the delicacy with which subjective sense and

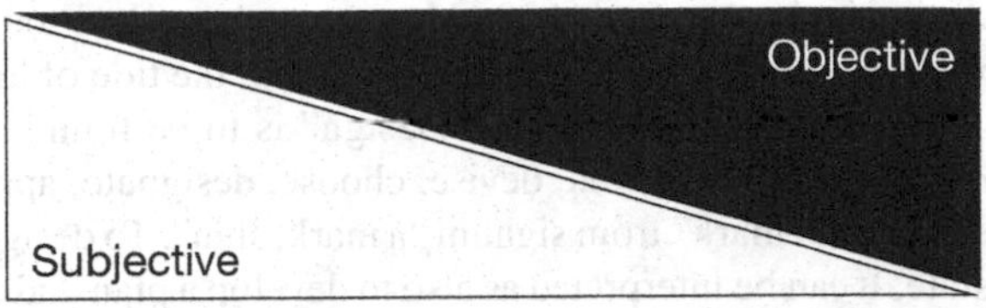

Fig. 1.1 Subjective–objective dichotomy

logic are engaged. We, designers, grasp design as an activity that puts the body into the reorganization of the pair: senses and logic. The nature of design is understood only through actual first-hand experiences, because no matter how much you study theories and concepts, they would be meaningless unless they are sublimated onto the design activity. It is not until theories are embodied as bodily experience that substantial design skills are acquired.

In everyday life, we see that sensing does not yield to logic. Sensing in others is not easy to understand; even in ourselves, it is not easy to explain. It becomes clear only as an intrinsic part of life. As Krippendorff (2005) mentioned, "since we cannot observe others' senses, we have no direct access to the meanings they construct and no direct way of knowing why they see the world as they do" (p. 55). But why do we have logic and the senses contrasted as though they were dichotomized? The sense–logic conflict can be construed as the subjective–objective dichotomy.

Lakoff and Johnson (1980) state that "whereas scientific truth, rationality, precision, fairness, and impartiality are allied as objectivism, the emotion, intuitive insight, imagination, humaneness, art, and a higher truth are allied as subjectivism" (p. 189). From person to person and from culture to culture, the ratio of objectivism and subjectivism governed in everyday life is varied (Fig. 1.1). However, in modern society as a whole, "the realms of science, law, government, journalism, morality, business, economics, and scholarship" seem underpinned by objectivism (Lakoff and Johnson 1980, p. 189).

As science becomes more influential through technology in human life, we can find some reactions against imbalanced situations historically. For example, when the industrial revolution in England became dominant through large-scale machine production, poets, artists and social thinkers reacted against the machinery tide, in what art historians call the "Arts and Crafts movement". It was the advent of the Romantic tradition as a reaction against a crude machine production system.

The Romantics positioned themselves as representing subjectivism and declared that science, reason, and technology had turned away from people and the natural environment. They further claimed that art and poetry were not produced by rationality, logic or reason but were "the spontaneous overflow of powerful feelings" (Lakoff and Johnson 1980, p. 192) and suggested "a return to nature as a way for people to recover their humanity" (also p. 192). It is no exaggeration to say that these reactions can be understood as "the origin of design" or "the advent of design".

We are beings located just here and now between the future and the past. We can look forward to the future lying ahead of us, but also there is a history of design behind us. In the following section, the period from the advent of the concept of design in the Arts and Crafts Movement through to today is briefly reviewed, so that we can see a perspective of design within the tide of history.

The first use of the term "Design" is to be found in the 1540s, from the Latin, *designare* "to mark out, devise, choose, designate, appoint". It is from de- "out" + signare "to mark" from signum "a mark, sign". To design is to bring order to a chaotic state. It can be interpreted as also to develop a plan and conceive it in mind in "order" to visualize or form.

There are a number of discussions about the origin of the concept of design based on different perspectives and disciplines from culture to culture. A thousand designers and scholars would define a hundred ways of description in terms of design. For example, some of them would argue that "design" originated as the human species' use of technology began with the conversion of natural resources into simple tools such as stones 200,000 years ago, or the prehistorical discovery of the ability to control fire before 1,000,000 BC (Crump 2001; UNESCO 2011). It can be also said to be the origin of technology. Another example is cave paintings from 32,000 years ago (Clottes 2003). They were supposed to be a sort of "design", used as a communication tool. Further, in relation to communication tools, western calligraphy in the Bible probably played a role to bring order for communication. Especially, Johannes Gutenberg (1398–1468) invented the printing system with movable types, which made possible mass-producing different typographic designs and relatively rapid printings (Martin 1995).

There is also an accepted view that explains the origin of design as emergence of an established profession after the industrial revolution in England (Pevsner 1991). Design or designer as a profession had a responsibility in society and played a role to contribute to society. That means that the professional way of thinking of design was recognized in society. This book adopts this view of the origin of design in the origin of industrial design. The following sections discuss the history of design and the advent of design, based on this view, in the origination of a way of perceiving design in a society.

1.4 Arts and Crafts

According to the art historian Nikolaus Pevsner, in his book "Pioneers of modern design" (1991), the "design", as we know it today, emerged from the two profound social thinkers: William Morris (1834–1896) and John Ruskin (1819–1900). They were proponents of social thought and the founders of the Arts and Crafts Movement. During the era, John Ruskin and William Morris with much respect and fondness for their own culture must have been concerned about the decline in sense of beauty. They alleged that people had lost something in achieving this new mass production.

The sensibilities, which had been nurtured by skilled craftsmen's work against the concealing background of sophisticated European culture, rather clearly emerged as a result of their protest against industrialization (Hara 2007). Lakoff and Johnson (1980) introduced Wordsworth and Coleridge as symbolizing romanticism, in that "they gladly left reason, science, and objectivity to the dehumanized empiricists and exalted imagination as a more humane means of achieving a higher truth, with emotion as a natural guide to self-understanding" (p. 192).

Although this romanticism or Ruskin's and Morris's Arts and Crafts Movement reinforced anti-science attitudes, with both defending the renaissance of the skilled craftsman practices and taking critical attitude towards the harmful impacts of machine production, their disputes vanished into the mainstream of the era and were unable to draw enough movement to block the rapid changes of the industrial revolution or to decelerate society's alteration (Pevsner 1991; Hara 2007). The result of this separation between the romantic position and rapid industrialization was the isolation of the romanticists from the mainstream of society. By willingly accepting subjectivism, the romantic position made distinct "the dichotomy between truth and reason, on the one hand, and art and imagination, on the other" (Lakoff and Johnson 1980, p. 192).

The romantic tradition in terms of "design" could be described as the strong negative reaction of aesthetic sensibility against the callousness and prematurity concealing in the industrial system, which was forcefully destroying a sensitive and reflective way of living in the environment. As Hara (2007) pointed out, this then provoked the concept of design, or the origination of its way of perceiving of design in society. The romanticism movement in the era led by poets, artists and philosophers is a clear symbol of how humanity and science were opposed. Their sensitive views that the source of quality of life exists in the relationship between design and everyday life were handed down to the design thinkers in later eras, who supported the design movement. This was the main source of the concept of design, which went on to have meaningful impacts on society after all. This design thinking emerged by taking the appearance of crude, machine-made consumable products as a starting point.

So, it is clear that "design" originally had a social aspect. Hara (2007) refers to the Kelmscott Press and says that "*their spirited drive in demonstrating—not through theory but through real objects—an antithesis to the doltish objects manufactured by the clumsy machine is still intense and ardent enough to unsettle the sensibilities of today's designers; we still succumb to its beauty*" (Hara 2007, p. 417). In similar ways to the effects of the industrial revolution, society has been newly transformed by the rapid development and spread of information technology. Different kinds of pain have arisen in the recent information society as if we were repeating history and turning back to the era of Ruskin and Morris. This reminds us of the origin of design in various arts movements in civil society. It is a good time to re-consider the origin of modernistic design thought.

1.5 Industrialization and the Bauhaus

The industrialized system, denied by Ruskin and Morris, was positively recognized through the activities of the Bauhaus. Hara (2007, p. 420) emphasized that "John Ruskin and William Morris nurtured the seeds; the art movements of the early twentieth century cultivated the soil; consequently, it was on the soil of Germany that design put forth small buds in the form of the Bauhaus". Their concept of design was accomplished by integrating the modernism movement and the mass production system. The Bauhaus represents a leading art and design movement in the realization of the concept of design. In 1919, the Bauhaus was established as a school of design and is positioned as a historically prominent art and design movement that began in Weimar, Germany (Droste and Gossel 2006). Its rich activities were practiced for only 14 years. They was forced to close for political reasons in 1933 (https://www.uni-weimar.de, accessed in December 2011).

After the period from the Movement originated by Ruskin and Morris through to the activities of the Bauhaus, a new phase of art movements emerged across the world. Although those emergences, approaches and expressions varied from culture to culture in different countries and with different ideologies, they appeared in every area of Europe and in every field of art and design such as Cubism, Art Nouveau, the Vienna Secession, Futurism, Dadaism, De Stijl, Constructivism, Absolutism, Modernism and so on (Pevsner 1991). In the same historical moment, a variety of concepts for the arts were brought to the surface by the art movements of the beginning of the twentieth century and were reorganized by the Bauhaus.

The Bauhaus was an ambitious and repeated trial-and-error approach to completely deconstruct all the vocabularies of the historical decorative arts of the past, such as adornment expressions and modes, and cliquish, crusted and patrician tastes. All kinds of elements in relation to art expressions were speculatively simplified into sensual such primitive elements as dot, line, shape, colour, texture, volume, plane, space, and such principles as balance, proportion, contrast, pattern, rhythm and so on, which could not be reduced to further primitives (Droste and Gossel 2006). It was the Bauhaus that deconstructed ornamental and aristocratic art styles and forms into simple elements, filtered out, arranged and ordered those elements.

The Bauhaus is the result of the deconstruction of styles and forms of arts movements, and the integration of all elements and activities carried out by such many talents as Walter Gropius (1883–1969), Jahannes Itten (1888–1967), Hannes Meyer (1889–1954), Paul Klee (1879–1940), Laslo Moholy-Nagy (1895–1946) and Wassily Kandinsky (1866–1943) (Pevsner 1991; Droste and Gossel 2006). As many historians and designers have mentioned, it is not easy to characterize the Bauhaus philosophy by any single aspect. It was a compilation of activities attempted by a large number of designers, artists, architects and philosophers.

Whether from Ruskin and Morris or from the Bauhaus, design has a romantic aspect. The concept of design was originally conceived and developed on the premise of idealistic social ethics. Ruskin and Morris detested being controlled by an economy in which human life was filled up with crude machine productions. The development of the Bauhaus was made possible by the existence of the social-democratic government in Weimar; "it can be said that the social-democratic trend fostered the Bauhaus way of thinking" (Hara 2007, p. 422). As art and design historians mentioned (Pevsner 1991; Hara 2007), the machine production and the power of the economy engaged and began to drive the world in the second half of the twentieth century. At a time when design was supposed to be the development of blossoming of ability, it ended up being buffeted by economic pressures. Hara (2007) pointed out that "The purer the concept, the less able it is to live up to its ideal, within the intensity of rapid and accelerating economic principle" (p. 421). This also reminds us of the way in which the poets, artists and philosophers of the romantic position were estranged from mainstream society (Lakoff and Johnson, 1980).

Modernist designers, architects and philosophers, who emigrated to escape the 2nd world war, brought the concept of design to the wider world. Walter Gropius (1883–1969) joined Harvard University in the United States, Mies van der Rohe (1886–1969) was invited to the Illinois Institute of Technology in the U.S., Laszlo Moholy-Nagy (1895–1946) established the New Bauhaus in Chicago (Droste and Gossel 2006).

Even though "the social democratic-tinged thought of the Bauhaus" (Hara 2007, p. 425) fed into the concept of design, the Bauhaus-based design thought in an economically developed culture evolved with the development of pragmatic methods that support its economic development in the United States. This pragmatism influenced "design" in the western bloc culture in which the United States is the driving force behind the world economy. Recently, we see that this stream has been flowing ever faster and becoming a mainstream of our society, not least through the market penetration of new interactive technologies such as mobile phone, tablets and car interiors.

1.6 Design as Marketing Tool

The evolution of design after the closing of the Bauhaus differs from society to society depending on the circumstances of its national politics and economical system, for example, between Japan, the United States and Europe. Our planet has long been revolving on the blindly accepted standard of economic might. In a world in which economic power dominates the majority of our belief, science became a powerful tool to predict economical changes, in turn to preserve economic might. This is one reason why science has largely kept away from everyday concerns. Science became a tool for exploring economic opportunities, and design was exposed to pressure to be scientific. After the 2nd world war, the scientific aspect of design clearly had its direction merged with that of technological and economical mastery which itself accrued much of the prestige of science, rather than its origin in scientific thinking.

In this situation, innovation by design has tended to be interpreted as a way to increase people's appetite for consumption. So design in current commercialized societies is a strategic tool to motivate consuming and spending, and design has responded by taking on the role of producing continual changes to product appearance and interfaces based on novel technologies. All kinds of consumer products have made noisy claims by changing their appearances and stimulating consumer desires.

After the 2nd world war, the countries of the western bloc (and Japan) had industries preparing for post-war revitalization and economic growth, and the assiduous workers to take on the responsibility of that growth. It can be said that industries and design in capitalist society also contributed in large part to standardization and mass production as well. A clear example of design that contributed to standardization and mass production is Japanese industrial design. Japanese industrial design was directed towards rapidly growing the economy, not towards improving the already mature consciousness of higher aesthetic and cultural life, and turned towards the direction of economic growth in order to recover from the devastating damage of war, rather than towards the true nature of our aesthetic life (Hara 2007). In such industrial design, the identity of design and designer is subdued. Rather, the design and designer have to support and accurately reflect the strategy of the corporations to make profits. On the other hand, Japanese design rationally and skillfully combined materials and technology in industrial design responses to the requirements of the civilized lifestyle. It brought high product quality in the longer term, but design remained the servant of the market.

Design has today become a tool for presenting the latest innovations of technology in a way that stimulates economic growth. Our society has stepped into a complicated period of disturbance, marked by the striking progress of ICT (information and communication technology). People believed this new technology of the computer could dramatically increase the quality of human life, and the business world has reacted to potential business opportunities in that computerized future. And yet technology is so imperfectly applied to our everyday life. Obviously, people are silent about claiming imperfect technological progress. Earlier, the Romantics asserted that "science, reason, and technology had alienated man from himself and his natural environment" (Lakoff and Johnson 1980, p. 192). Now ICT is alienating man from himself by the way it is designed. Hence the need for this book.

Hara (2007) refers to people in modern information society and says that:

"*It may be that deeply seated in the consciousness of our contemporaries is an obsession of a sort, to the effect that those who contradicted the machine civilization were thought of as lacking in foresight and were looked down upon*" (Hara 2007, p. 430). People, especially in HCI, may think that the information society should evolve more slowly and take the time to be matured rationally, in the light of repeated empirical observation. But as the Romantics experienced earlier, the information society has no time for those who can't keep up the pace.

Prominent products designed by the talent of individual designers guarantee quality and originality. The product reputation for superiority is then maintained as a "brand" (Hara 2007). The concept of "brand" has been further developed and studied as a methodology within marketing, corporate management and strategic advertisement, especially in the United States (American Marketing Association 2011). One of the many roles of design today is to strategically incorporate such information as corporate identity and brand management into corporate business (Wheeler et al. 2006).

The United States originated this process, having already been the first country to develop sophisticated management methods for more profitable business. And yet we can find distinctive characteristics of German and Italian design, for example, Braun and Olivetti. Olivetti has kept higher originality and excellence in communicating its brand image through design. It is not well known that the Bauhaus graduate Alexander Schawinski (1904–1979) contributed to Olivetti's graphic and product design from 1933 to 1936 (Baroni and Vitta 2003). The Braun brand is the result of high-attitude human factor researches, in collaboration with the Ulm School of Design that inherited the Bauhaus philosophy.

1.7 Design as Integrated Knowledge and Skill

Just as European craftsmen showed their skilled performance, European designers take pride in and responsibility for their skilled craftsman-like design work. Historically, the spirit of well-trained craftspeople lies behind European manufacturing. The Bauhaus education system basically gave co-teaching lessons with a professor and a master craftsman. According to Whitford (1993):

> …Bauhaus not only because it specifically referred to bauen (building, construction) – but also because of its similarity to the word Bauhütte, the medieval guild of builders and stonemasons out of which Freemasonry sprang. The Bauhaus was to be a kind of modern Bauhütte, therefore, in which craftsmen would work on common projects together, the greatest of which would be buildings in which the arts and crafts would be combined. (Whitford 1993, p. 32)

In Germany, the Ulm School of Design (1953–1968) took over the Bauhaus philosophy (Krippendorff 2006). We can find the prominent design results in the education program at the Ulm School of Design. German quality products symbolized by Braun AG are typical example of the results of the principles of the education program. It was the result of intellectual research into human factors in which the philosophy of the Bauhaus was inherited by the Ulm (Krippendorff 2005). The principle of the Ulm School of Design positioned design within integrated research disciplines that include the field of architecture, environment, product form, visual communication and information (Spitz 2002).

At the Ulm School of Design, Louis Henry Sullivan's dictum "form follows function", replaced as "Functionalism", served as "a principle for rational justifications of designs" (Krippendorff 2005, p. 298). Max Bill (1908–1994) organized the design program and refined Sullivan's dictum as four functions: technical, material, production and aesthetic (Spitz 2002). They provide, not simply traditional design knowledge and practice with colour and form, but also philosophy, aesthetics, human factors, physics, information technology based on integrated formative science, premised on a crossover to science. Their approaches were apparently scientific. However, they fell prey to industries, which circulated the idea that the success of the Ulm was because their designs defeated obsolete designs described as though they were unscientific and indefensible (Krippendorff 2005). This apparently scientifically objective design was well matched to the needs of post-war industries in order to replace "out of date" products.

As a phenomenon that deserves special mention in the design history of the world, a design movement called "postmodern", originating in Italy, sparked off in the '80s. The movement spread across such disciplines as architecture, interior design and product design. The present thesis does not intend to discuss the philosophy of postmodernism. It is not easy to philosophically define what is postmodern in architecture and design. Postmodern in architecture and design seems a stray thread at the end of modernism, hence we are still in the modernist era.

Almost all the objects produced these days are comprised of basic elements such as colour, form and texture entrusted to the rational and lucid modernist process that aims to integrate those elements. In other words, "Design" in a broad sense has aimed to be the pursuit of an integrated balance of the human mind through the rational process of making things. Therefore, the activities of design can be understood as the willingness to interpret the meaning of human life through the integrated design process. This can be referred to as design as social thought.

Design originates in society but not self-expression. From the perspective of daily life, design offers a criticism of civilization. Not that this is anything new. Design has been critical from the beginning, as can be seen from the Bauhaus and the Arts and Crafts Movement. The concept of design has always kept a position directly adjacent to this awareness and rationality through social thought. In this sense, the entire world needs a rationally balanced design, which integrates flexibly issues on every front: a truly fair economy, resource conservation, sustainable environment, mutual respect for culture and so on.

1.8 Interaction Design: Designing Computer-Based Artefacts

Information technology continues with an advanced edge far away from everyday life and has been growing exponentially, beyond the limit that can be comprehended or made sense of by a human being. For example, at one time, car owners could understand the whole system of owned cars. They could fix and repair their own cars. Since more and more information technology has been integrated into the system, a level of complexity unmanageable by an owner has been created. The unstable information systems rooted in an unsteady ground system have rapidly evolved but are weak and at risk of failure. People have been forced into being in our current unstable information society.

Does design have to cling closely to new technologies? Is design a servant to the economy or technology? In our recent industrial and information society, design has played a role as the rational and efficient pilot, steering towards optimal objects and environments that improve daily life. Designers fulfil the responsibility with the best intention to pursue better solutions, in every technological progress that reveals a new possibility for creating new products or services.

Designers today have realized immeasurable possibilities for design in the shared scenes of our everyday lives, not simply in the new novel fruits brought by technology. The combination of technology, information and communication let designers begin to rethink the possibilities. This does not mean that they try to replace the outdated communication media with new media (Hara 2007). But they create more positive outcomes through accepting the former media. Such communication media as E-mail, mobile phones and social networking service have been rapidly popularizing, yet we are happy when we receive a handwritten card. The substantial texture and original calligraphy on the card arouse our curiosity. Design is a true profession without relying on one-sided ways of using either old or new media. Rather, design has a role in exploring the true nature of media, but design is not a servant of media. Design and design research should not take part in making what's new today look old tomorrow; otherwise, we have to seek what's new everlastingly.

Recent designers and researchers have focused on the profoundness and intricacy of the quality of information and communication perceivable when all senses become integrated. Tangible interaction, haptic interfaces, and augmented reality in HCI are typical examples of new communication media integrating several senses. This shows that people have realized the importance of the very delicate human senses rather than conceptual thought, in the forefront of technology. We integrate our communication with the environment via our diverse sensory perception. We then can comfort and satisfy essential human life. This kind of design is not trying to draw the audience's consciousness with an attractive expression, but having the expression permeate into the sensual perception. This is design that is very modest and disappears from our perception. It tangibly exists before we even realize it's there.

This brief overview of design history tells us that the origin of design was not merely an activity to adorn outer surfaces, and design is not an activity that draws customers' consciousness with catchy presentations. Rather, design is a subtle activity to discover new issues in everyday life. It is the creativity that repeatedly derives modest ideas from partial fragments of our shared everyday life. In other words, design is an activity that creates empathy among human beings through our common values. The more delicate and subtly shared, the more powerful the empathy sensed. The empathy is sometimes called, for example, shared feeling or shared reality. The resources of design exist only as small minor objects and behaviours in everyday life. This seems to be what Romantic people and the Bauhaus had pursued. The future of a human-centred design science lies beyond the rational pursuit of the human being, in the integration of people, technology and science.

For nearly 60 years, we have seen a vast amount of often successful development of digital technologies, not only the traditional desktop personal computers, but also computers incorporated into devices, so-called embedded computing such as smartphones, car-based systems and even kitchen appliances. Many disciplines and researchers have tried to conceptualize the history of interaction with computers, the historical development of user interfaces. There are many points of view to discuss it from, such as the technological view, political view, psychological view, social view and so on (Card et al. 1983; Dourish 2001; Grudin 1990). Dourish (2001) presented "the stages in the historical development of user interfaces in terms of the different history sets of human skills they are designed to exploit" (p. 5). Electrical, symbolic, textual and graphical forms of interaction were identified.

When the symbolic forms of machine language were used, the users were mostly programmers who had special knowledge and skills and were willing to use machine language for industrial use or in research laboratories. The computer was not seen in the commercial mass market at this stage. However, as Dourish (2001, p. 10) describes it:

> the textual stage drew upon language much more explicitly than before, and at the same time it was accompanied by a transition to a new model of computing, in which a user would actually sit in front of a computer terminal entering commands and reading responses. (Dourish 2001, p. 10)

The so-called Command Line Interface (CLI) is one kind of interaction with a computer operating system by typing commands to manage specific tasks. This method of instructing a computer to perform a given task obviously requires explicit knowledge, which is articulated, and can be expressed and recorded as words, numbers, codes, and mathematical and scientific formulas. Since then, the computer began to stretch out into society, being more inexpensive and smaller, and came into common use particularly for office workers. It gradually became the Personal Computer (PC). This interface evolved to be more intuitive and easier to use for general users, not only office workers. The evolution is well known to us as the transition from textual user interface to Graphical User Interface (GUI).

It is often discussed that whereas CLI is classical and inconvenient, GUI is intuitive and easier to use. However, there are indeed advantages and disadvantages. End users prefer to use GUIs, but CLIs are often used by programmers and system administrators in engineering and scientific environments, and by technically advanced personal computer users. Actually, the CLI continues to co-evolve with GUIs. The development of graphical interaction techniques brought a specific kind of model of the interface. Users directly operate explicitly represented objects, which is known as direct manipulation. The designers sought to evoke explicitly people's knowledge of office work to help them understand the operation of the computer.

Since the development of digital technologies progressed, information systems have become complicated. A large number of disciplines are also involved in the system development process. The whole system is often not understandable and not easier to use for users. Therefore, the concept of *human-centred design* or *user-centred design* has been introduced to emphasize the importance of involving users and incorporating users' aspects and contexts of use into the design process.

The more important users' viewpoint becomes in system development, the more the participatory design approach has adapted to system development. Especially, Scandinavian participatory design has more than 30 years of history. Participatory design became a more and more integral part of the system development process. Disciplines including designers, managers and workers in the participatory design process investigate and represent the skills and experiences of users, so that the design and organizational implementation of computer systems can be improved (Schuler and Namioka 1993).

However, user-centred concerns are not what decides what is a successful interaction design. The success of interaction design is currently measured by how well a product sells and how elegantly conflicts between aesthetics, production, usability and costs are resolved in the design. In such a situation, there are concerns about the uncritical drive of technological progress, when technology is always (if implicitly) assumed to be good and capable of solving any problem. And that the technological solution that sells best, with its particular repertoire of interactions, is just what is needed in the here and now. But can it really be so?

When economies continue to grow, the designers' role becomes one of promoting the consumption bias inherent in consumerist culture. Designers are extolled as if the commercial success of products is mostly due to design. And during economic downturns they are required to stimulate the economy in various attractive ways that encourage people to consume more interactive products. A possible effect on designers themselves is that they become distressed, seeing themselves as only menial servants of the profit motive. Recent designs in relation to information–communication technology are strongly tied to the marketplace and have left little room for profound contemplation on the cultural function of interactive systems, whereas cultural speculation and critical thought about the fine arts and architecture have been part and parcel of their existence for some time. Looking for a remedy for this situation was a major stimulus for the writing of this book.

1.9 Primitive Interaction Design

To find inspiration for the new view of design presented in this book, and to change attitudes about designing, we have looked beyond conventional design to the methodological playgrounds of anthropology, mythology, theology, science, ethics and art. Building on some of the ideas introduced in our earlier book "Human-Experiential Design of Presence in Everyday Blended Reality: Living in the Here and Now" (Waterworth and Hoshi 2016), we set out in later chapters to explore what we call primitive interaction design, to release designers from the spell they are under and, through them, the people who buy the products. A consideration of the spiritual dimension, and of myth, of emptiness and of the unconscious should come as a revelation to the profession and inspire new ways that design can make technology more meaningful and relevant to our lives, embodying primitive elements of human experience and understanding. This potentially opens up design to everyone and grounds interaction designers more in the human experience of being.

Primitive Interaction Design is founded on experiential design. We call it "primitive" in many senses of the word, including the following:

- Primitive as pre-linguistic
- Primitive interaction as unconscious interaction
  - Tangible presence
- Primitive as being
  - Mental being rather doing
- Primitives of human understanding
  - Image schemata
  - Human universals
- Primitive distinctions
  - Fullness and emptiness
- Primitives of experience
  - Bauhaus
  - Here and Now
- Primitive Art
  - Naïve or folk design.

Human-experiential design (HXD) is itself a relatively new approach to human-centred design, first presented in Waterworth and Hoshi (2016). The human-experiential approach incorporates bodily experiences into the process of developing interactive systems, and therefore fosters true universal design for everyone (since we all share fundamentally similar embodiment). It also provides an identification of a reframed categorization of humanity, which allows us to discover new aspects of the human and true human-centredness. Actual human beings have been lost within categorized humanity. HXD is based on the idea that we are neither customers/users nor

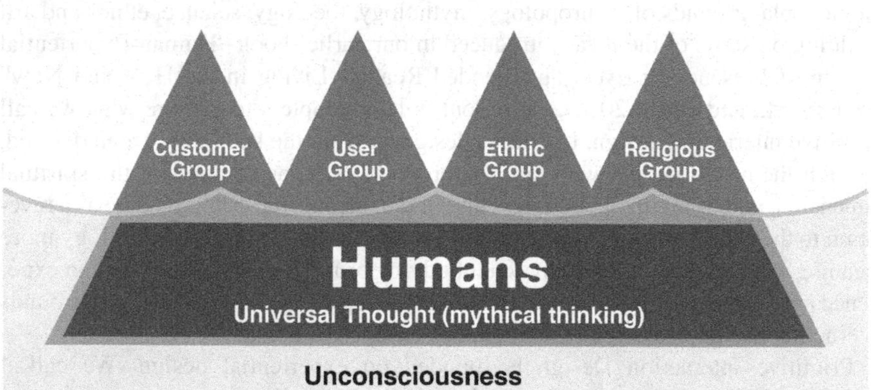

Fig. 1.2 Human-centredness

particular segmented groups, and certainly not predictable machines. HXD targets true human beings with a shared repertoire of primitive experiences that have evolved over thousands, even millions of years, through the mythical, nomadic and hunting ages to the present (Fig. 1.2).

1.10 Outline of the Book

1.10.1 Part 1—Motivations and Inspirations

In this chapter, we have discussed design, leading into the human aspect of design, what we have called human-experiential design, and the significance of HXD has been summarized. We raised some aspects of HXD which are further developed in the rest of the book, which lays out the roots and approach of primitive interaction designing in detail.

We start in Chap. 2 with Auguste Comte, who founded the doctrine of positivism, and proposed three phases that our quest for knowledge successively passes through: theological, metaphysical and scientific. He further claimed that we have reached the stage of scientific progress based on a linear progression through history. It is very difficult for design, in our current information age, to identify new goals if we accept this rigorously linear and monodirectional hypothesis of progress.

However, if we adopt a circular view of history, which is much closer to eastern philosophy, the point of arrival could also be the point of departure. Having gone through science, we find ourselves returning to a more mythical and savage stage. In our current era characterized by information society, the perception of the "untamed mind" is ever more important. How we interact now, with virtual reality, movies, images and tweets instead of texts, is indicative of this return to being, to the concrete.

In Chap. 2, we examine the way we interact(ed) based on this circular history view. We see the way forward from current design thinking to new mythical thinking. We then attempt to identify common attributes—or primitives—of ways of thinking and design in relation to untamed/savage/mythical minds. We discuss the significance of the untamed mind as applied to design thinking and show how designers with untamed minds can be advocates for alternative design mindsets in the years to come.

1.10.2 Part 2—Theories and Foundations

People today consider the thinking of so-called primitive people ("savages"), for example, mythical thought, to be inferior to scientific thinking. Lévi-Strauss defines the decisive contrast between "primitive" and "civilized" thinking. He argued that instead of "primitive" we should say "without writing" (Lévi-Strauss 1966, 2001).

People without writing use more of their sensory perceptions and have developed certain mental capacities of observation that civilized people have lost.

In Chap. 3, based on Levi-Strauss's work, we explore the characteristic patterns of mythological thought and its universality, shared among all mankind, as a complement to the more detailed and logical thought of modern "civilized" society. We see both methods towards acquiring knowledge, scientific and mythical thought, as equally valid in design. They are two ways of thinking, rather than two stages in the evolution of thought. We then attempt to apply mythical thought as an alternative design approach to the ordinary interaction design mindset.

Inspired by the suggestion of Hosoe (2006—A Trickster Approach to Interaction Design), we examine the cultural role of Trickster, which in some ways can be seen as parallelling a potential cultural/social role of a designer. The Trickster figure, found in several mythologies, is comprised of contradictory traits characterized by duality; for example, intelligence and foolishness, maliciousness and benevolence, clowning and heroism, Satan and saviour, disruption and creativeness, and so on (Lévi-Strauss 1966, 2001). The designer seen as trickster offers such catalysts as raising awareness, creating optimal conditions for a cultural paradigm shift or even introducing a fundamental meta-narrative into a particular culture.

We expand on the potential of drawing on what we call primitive interaction design through a consideration of the savage or untamed mind in the development of interactive systems for a range of application areas. We specifically argue for the importance of myth as a source of design creativity, and particularly the character Trickster as a designer role model—as a mediator between mythical and modern thought—an alternative for designers who have fallen under the spell of instrumental rationality.

Chapter 4 deals with the importance of emptiness. As Kenya Hara said, "emptiness is richer than fullness". Emptiness carries enormous promise but is also feared: we fill empty time and space with objects and sounds and phone calls and Facebook, because emptiness brings the uncertainty of unresolved possibilities—the very essence of creative potential. Emptiness, then, can be promising or threatening. As Nagarjuna, the early Buddhist philosopher taught, "Emptiness wrongly grasped is like picking up a poisonous snake by the wrong end".

We aim to explore the world of the senses from an experiential perspective, which has largely become a delusive world for science, suggesting that untamed minds are characterized by using more of their sensory perceptions to support certain mental capacities for observation that modern "tamed" people have lost. We relate this to the creation of interactive environments, especially emerging digital-physical blended spaces. This is an approach to designing spaces that resonates with the functional needs and minds of their users' activities by also maintaining a degree of emptiness, to be filled unconsciously with sensory aspects of experiences. We speculate that "Ma", the Japanese concept of space and emptiness, is an essential aspect of the successful design of such interactive environments. Further, we explore the possibilities for universal design via a view of the universality of mind in Zen philosophy and transpersonal psychology, emphasizing phenomenology and experiential ontology in terms of eight levels of consciousness.

The meaning of emptiness depends on the context, which refers to the conditions in which a situation or communication exists that make its meaning understandable. Perceptual meaning can be defined by how much the empty space is filled up with contextual cues. For example, such contextual cues as the surroundings, circumstances, environment, background or settings, or more specifically, weight, texture, smell, airflow, sound, light and shadow, may all contribute to a context that facilitates creativity through sensory experiences. By contrast, if a person is in a situation of fully conscious thought and explicit information—for example, absorbed in understanding a complex legal document—there is no space to be filled up with contextual cues (from the five sense faculties), and the. person is mentally absent from their current situation. The feeling of presence is in the timeless now, through sensory perceptions of objects and other features of the present environment.

Part of the unacknowledged design skill in creating successful artefacts and systems stems, ironically, from the fact that in the perception of empty space designers employ not only vision but also their other senses. Olfaction, shifts in temperature, humidity, light, shade, and colour work together, so as to enhance the person's whole body as a sensing organ. It is as if their sensory perceptions have developed certain mental capacities of observation. We explore this notion of emptiness and observation, initially from the perspective of Buddhist philosophy, and then discuss just how "emptiness" factors affect the experience of presence in design computer-mediated realities.

Most designers, like most other people, are generally limited by the unconscious cultural grip of living in their own particular world, a world of conceptual thought, judgment and belief, or a world of the remembered past and imagined future—in other words, an ideologically generated world. They are absorbing impressions into the internal world of their thoughts and imagination based on their cultural environment. This gives them a sense of self beyond the present moment. But it also produces a separation from the external world and breaks the natural flow of action that is based on constant activity while awake. When functioning smoothly, people act through largely unconscious motor behaviours, they attend to the here and now without thinking (much), and have a sense of almost complete absorption in what we call contextual emptiness, the external world of the present.

We move on to discuss the perception of emptiness from the perspective of Japanese culture, because in the West "emptiness" has different, more limited meanings, with only negative cultural associations such as boredom, meaninglessness and more generally a lack of anything valuable. Why has Japan produced a culture with such a different view of emptiness? The answer can be found in a concept familiar to every Japanese person: "MA". MA is universal and refers to both the interval, which gives shape to the whole, and the whole itself. In the second part of the chapter, we discuss the singularity and universality of MA in relation to design. The MA concept can be seen as the purest essence of distinctly Japanese thought. MA is time and space. The two cannot be considered separately. MA underlies almost everything and is an important component of communication. MA has no substantive meaning. Here, we will attempt to reveal the hidden semantics intrinsic to a work of MA.

In Japanese arts and architecture, MA epitomizes the dynamic balance between object and space, action and inaction, sound and silence, movement and rest. We explore why Japanese classic artists and architects historically have used MA as the consummate concept, while western arts have had little interest in MA, and why there is no general understanding of MA in western culture. We explore the principles and processes of creation in MA. MA can be described as a creative space, which opens and closes, swells and contracts as though it were endowed with unlimited functional flexibility.

Primitive interaction design emphasizes the experiential, not the ideological. This implies respecting the importance of the here and now to experience, since in fact all experience is in the here and now. The illusion of being in time (of experiencing time's passage) comes from thought and internal language—a narrative that demands retention of symbols in (working) memory to tell a story, rather than experiencing reality here and now. The passage of time is "perceived" in absence from the here and now, through conception, whereas presence can be said to be in the timeless now, through perception (Waterworth et al. 2015). Successful interaction design entails the kind of thoughtlessness or empty-headedness that leads to unconscious interaction.

Chapter 5 deals with the unconsciousness, both in interaction and in design. Although the ideal of seamless interaction is that people do not need to think how to use digital technology, design researchers and design practitioners have tended to focus on explicitly revealing problems and solving them. These are problems that they can physically see and linguistically discuss. Although this may involve questions of how to design for mostly unconscious interaction, it does not generally take into account that there are different levels of the world in our everyday life: overt and covert, implicit and explicit, things you can and do talk about and things you cannot and do not talk about. It is not just that people interact unconsciously and designers seek to achieve this as an aim, it is that there is such a thing as the unconscious, the submerged and unobserved fundament of our psychic existence. Beneath the clearly perceived, highly explicit surface phenomena, there lies a whole other world or even worlds. This applies equally to people interacting and designers (who are people too) designing. Once we understand this, it changes our view of human nature and how to design for and with it.

There is an aspect or theory of Buddhist philosophies and practice, emphasizing phenomenology and ontology through the interior lens of introspective and meditative practice. This is similar in some ways to Western phenomenological theories and epistemological idealism. However, the Buddhist position rejects western metaphysical idealism, for example, the immaterialism of Berkeley's (1685–1753) subjective idealism. Rather, it takes a consciousness- or mind-only position, with which recent representationalist theories of mind (e.g. Seigel 2014; Chalmers 2017) are surprisingly compatible. Representationalism posits that perception is awareness of what one has in front of one. Perceptual experience is a matter of representing objects, properties and relations in the mind (de Sá Pereira 2016). These views suggest that we are spectators of our own mental experiences.

1.10.3 Part 3—Design Untamed

In Part 3, we present our new design approach in more detail, presenting practical ideas, and concrete examples from our projects. First, we describe exactly how the interaction designer can be reconstructed as a savage or primitive designer, drawing on the theories and foundations presented in Part 2. Next, we outline design processes and methods that are available to carry out primitive interaction design, drawing on both instinct and intellect, including a way of adopting "bricolage" techniques and a way of capturing experiential aspects of interaction through a first-person phenomenological approach. We then present examples of primitive interaction design, allowing the reader to understand the processes applied in several different contexts, and the practical results.

As we have seen, the savage mind can be described as the thought of primitive people without writing. They desire to understand the world around them, its nature and society. They are thinkers and also handymen, using so-called *bricolage*, rather disinterested thinking and intellectual reasoning as a philosopher does, and to some extent a scientist. The term *bricolage* has also been used and discussed in many other fields, including anthropology, philosophy, critical theory, education, computer science and business (e.g. Louridas 1999; Markham 2017; Vallgårda and Fernaeus 2015).

Bricolage can be described as the creation of being, filled up with events and perceived with senses. On the other hand, science can be seen as the creation of systemized events, filled up with conceptual structure. Primitive design is in the integration of the two. Primitive designers create a structure out of the integration of external structure and events internalized with the body.

In Chap. 6, we attempt to identify design's role neither as an economically viable tool, nor as carried out by conventional mainstream designers. We examine the significance of "design as bricolage" and explore just how bricolage can provide an alternative for new ways of approach design and of using technology. Further, we argue for mythical thinking as an alternative creative mindset, opposed to *cultivated* systematic *thought* that systematically proceeds from goals to means.

By definition, people design and use tools. In this process, people are redesigned by their tools. As an example, consider early tool designs. Many archaeologists and anthropologists have argued that teardrop-shaped stone tools in the stone age were designed intellectually to achieve balance and perfection, and they were used as hand tools to make a better hand (Prestwich 1860; Gamble and Kruszynsky 2009; Colomina and Wigley 2016). According to these authors, the human hand is uniquely adapted to make and use tools; the inherited structure of the body has evolved through its technological extensions. The shape of the pieces of stone used for such tools reveals a regularity of shape that implies design, foresight and an intelligent purpose. Their tactile qualities, such as durability, hardness, weight and texture, would have been a determining medium for activating mankind towards the use of their hands. These sensory experiences stimulated their hands and minds and became the driving force of the stone age.

Some scientists and modernists would claim that there is an immense difference between today's people and these ancient (primitive) people. However, the activities of the latter show intellect and logical reasoning, and the historical difference is only one of degree. In ancient burial grounds, geometric engraving and ornamental beads discovered in Africa and the Middle East show that human creativity does not simply mean the ability to make and use tools. Colomina and Wigley (2016) suggest that ornaments and necklaces dating from between 135,000 and 120,000 BC were used to generate and share information, not just as attractive displays. This is an early example of the human ability to externalize thoughts in symbolic forms used as communication media.

The primitive design method places *design attitude* at the core of the interaction design process along with *ways of understanding* (observation and analysis) and *interaction space* (design and prototypical synthesis). Early human artefacts such as shaped stones, ornaments and necklaces were designed in ways that took them beyond material function. They were shared between groups and even between generations in a process that involved tacitly shared knowledge as part of the collective social unconsciousness of early societies. Taking account of this, the designer as savage is guided by a sense of values underlying such a process, such as *grace, conscientiousness, accuracy* and *simplicity* through minor variations and improvisation, which can also be described as creating solutions for a problem to be solved out of immediately available found objects.

In Chap. 7, we move on from considering the attitude of the primitive designer and sketch out some methods behind the primitive approach to designing interactive systems. These are:

- Capturing experiences by applying interpretive phenomenological analysis
- Techniques for maintaining necessary emptiness
- Actively promoting doing as being, unconscious design and interaction consequences
- Approaching design as bricolage, for example, using morphogenetic prototyping

The methods described are aimed at understanding the shape and the details of lived human experiences of people with artefacts. Our brief earlier review of anthropological, archaeological and design aspects of primitive people has shown that the behaviour of making stone tools, designing tools and designing interactions must trigger the mindfulness to improve the doing (through interaction) in designing utilitarian aesthetics. People's creative urges are evoked by interacting with tools (artefacts), and people are altered by their interactions with technology. Interaction and people produce each other socially, culturally and as-if physically. Put another way, interactive artefacts are not mere extensions of the human body, they are part of the constitution of the body necessary to be human in today's external reality.

Primitive interaction design is the act of externalization, not just knowledge in the brain. It helps to evoke a new sense of the interior, for without an outside there can be no inside. Artefact, body and mind are inseparable. Thinking should not be regarded as just a mindset in your head. Thoughts are partly the result of the gestures of externalization that potentially also invite new modes of thought. Thoughts only occur in the interaction between inside and outside.

Interpretive phenomenological analysis is presented as a way of understanding key experiential aspects of user intentions and activities as well as the interactions that may support (or hinder) them. We discuss how the primitive approach to design and our phenomenological analysis method complement each other, for example, showing how the method can help unveil meanings concealed behind human unconscious behaviours, as well as how observing and discussing interactions can clarify design expectations.

Drawing on insights derived from our phenomenological analysis method, morphogenetic prototyping (McGinley et al. 2018) is introduced as a practical primitive design method for actively exploring interaction possibilities. When a primitive design space is successfully functioning, relevant stakeholders such as designers, clients, engineers and so on can behave within it using largely unconscious motor behaviour and have a sense of absorption in contextual emptiness, the external world of the present. This means that they are attending to the here and now and not to the intricacies of an unnatural design tool interface. The users in the space behave as if they were both sacred and lewd bricoleurs, re-enacting trickster myths. In Chap. 8, we present this and other examples of primitive interaction design methods in action.

The final chapter of the book sums up and concludes the book as well as providing speculations for future developments. We conclude by outlining the expected contributions of our approach, seen as a way forward that opens new perspectives on interaction design, perspectives which will help us address the societal challenges facing us.

References

American Marketing Association (2011) https://www.marketingpower.com/Pages/default.aspx. Accessed 27 Dec 2011

Baroni D, Vitta M (2003) Storia Del Design Grafico Milan. Longanesi

Benyon D (2002) Representations in human-computer systems development cognition. Technol Work 4(3):180–196

Card SK, Moran TP, Newell A (1983) The psychology of human-computer interaction. Lawrence Erlbaum Associates Inc., Mahwah, NJ

Chalmers DJ (2017) The virtual and the real. Disputatio 9:309–352

Chalmers M (1996) Interface design: more craft than science? Paper presented at the 5th international workshop on interfaces for database systems, Edinburgh, UK

Clottes J (2003) Chauvet cave: the art of earliest times. University of Utah Press

Colomina B, Wigley M (2016) Are we human? Note on an archaeology of design. Lars Muller Publisher, Zurich, Switzerland

Crump T (2001) A brief history of science. Constable

Dourish P (2001) Where the action is: the foundation of embodied interaction. The MIT Press, Cambridge, MA

Droste M, Gossel P (2006) Bauhaus, Taschen basic art series. Taschen GmbH

de Sá Pereira RH (2016) Combining the representational and the relational view. Philos Stud 173(12):3255–3269

Fetaji M, Loskoska S, Fetaji B, Ebibi M (2007) Investigating human computer interaction issues in designing efficient virtual learning environments. Paper presented at the BCI 2007, Sofia, Bulgaria
Gamble C, Kruszynski RJE (2009) Joseph Prestwich and the Stone that shattered the time barrier. Antiquity 83(320):461–475
Grudin J (1990) The computer reaches out: the historical continuity of interface design. Paper presented at the human factors in computing systems CHI'90
Hara K (2007) Designing design. Lars Muller Publishers, Baden, Switzerland
Hosoe I (2006) A trickster approach to interaction design, theories and practice. In: Bagnara S, Smith GC (eds) Interaction design. Lawrence Erlbaum Associates, Mahwah, NJ, pp 311–322
Krippendorff K (2005) The semantic turn: a new foundation for design. CRC Press, Taylor & Francis Group, Boca Raton, FL
Krippendorff K (2006) The semantic turn: A new foundation for design. ARTIFACT-ROUTLEDGE 1(11):51
Lakoff G, Johnson M (1980) Metaphors we live by Chicago. The University of Chicago Press
Lévi-Strauss C (1966) The savage mind. University of Chicago Press, Chicago, Illinois
Lévi-Strauss C (2001) Myth and meaning. Routledge, London.
Long J, Dowell J (1989) Conceptions of the discipline of HCI: craft, applied science, and engineering. Paper presented at the the fifth conference of the BCS HCI SIG Nottingham, UK
Louridas P (1999) Design as bricolage: anthropology meets design thinking. Des Stud 20(6):517–535
Markham A (2017) Bricolage a keyword in remix studies, Jan 4, 2017. Annette Markham. https://annettemarkham.com/2017/01/bricolage-a-keyword-in-remix-studies/. Accessed 7 Mar 2017
Martin H-J (1995) The history and power of writing. University of Chicago Press. ISBN: 9780226508368
McGinley T, Hoshi K, Gruber P, Haddy S, Zavoleas Y, Tan L, Blaiklock D (2018) A Katana design experience. In Naweed A, Wardaszko M, Leigh E, Meijer S (eds) Intersections in simulation and gaming. ISAGA 2016, SimTecT 2016. Lecture notes in computer science, 10711. Springer, Cham
Norman DA (2007) The design of future things: author of the design of everyday things, 1st edn. Basic Books
Pevsner N (1991) Pioneers of modern design: from William Morris to Walter Gropius. Penguin, London
Plass JL (1998) Design and evaluation of the user interface of foreign language multimedia software: a cognitive approach. Lang Learn Technol 2(1):40–53
Prestwich J (1860) On the occurrence of flint implements associated with the remains of animals of extinct species in beds of a Late Geological Period in France at Amiens and Abbeville and in England at Hoxne, paper read May 26, 1859. Philosoph Trans R Soc Lond 150:294
Rosner DK (2009) Considering craftsmanship. Paper presented at the Posters presented at the iConference 2009
Schuler D, Namioka A (1993) Participatory design: principles and practices. CRC Press
Siegel S (2014) Affordances and the contents of perception. In: Brogaard B (ed) Does perception have content? Oxford University Press, Oxford
Spitz R (2002) The Ulm School of Design—a view behind the foreground. Edition Axel Menges
UNESCO (2011) Fossil Hominid Sites of Sterkfontein, Swartkrans, Kromdraai, and Environs. https://whc.unesco.org/pg.cfm?cid=31&id_site=915. Accessed 25 Sept 2011
Vallgårda A, Fernaeus Y (2015) Interaction design as a bricolage practice. In: Proceedings of the ninth international conference on tangible, embedded, and embodied interaction, pp 173–180
Waterworth J, Hoshi K (2016) Human-experiential design of presence in everyday blended reality: living in the here and now. Springer, Switzerland
Waterworth JA, Waterworth EL, Riva G, Mantovani F (2015) Presence: form, content and consciousness. In: Lombard M, Biocca F, Freeman J, IJsselsteijn W, Schaevitz RJ (eds) Immersed in media: telepresence theory, measurement & technology. Springer. ISBN: 978-3-319-10189-7

Wheeler AR, Richey RG, Tokkman M, Sablynski CJ (2006) Retaining employees for service competency: The role of corporate brand identity. J Brand Manag 14(1–2):96–113
Whitford F (1993) The Bauhaus: masters & students by themselves. Overlook Pr
Wright P, Blythe M, McCarthy J (2006) User experience and the idea of design in HCI. Interactive systems. Des Specifi Verifi 3941(1–14)

Chapter 2
Being Through Interaction

I sing the body electric,
The armies of those I love engirth me and I engirth them,
They will not let me off till I go with them, respond to them,
And discorrupt them, and charge them full with the charge of the soul.
Walt Whitman, *Leaves of Grass* (1855)

Abstract Auguste Comte claimed that we have reached the stage of scientific progress based on a linear progression through history. It is very difficult for design, in our current information age, to identify new goals if we accept this linear and monodirectional hypothesis of progress. In this chapter, we examine the way we interact(ed) based on a circular view of history, indicating a return from intellectual doing and moving further towards being. Being through interaction is a consequence of the turn to the tangible in HCI, which reflects a sense of presence (of being) in a digital world, through interaction, that is essentially the same as our sense of presence in the physical world. We consider the importance of subjective time to the nature of being and discuss how designers can design to affect this. We present and compare dimensions of mind and of interaction, pointing to the parallels and the directions in which being through interaction is taking us. Finally, we present some of the main challenges for the primitive interaction design approach.

2.1 Being and Time

Auguste Comte, who founded the doctrine of positivism, proposed three phases that our quest for knowledge successively passes through; theological, metaphysical and scientific. He further claimed that we have reached the stage of scientific progress based on a linear progression through history (Fig. 2.1). It is very difficult for design, in our current information age, to identify new goals if we accept this rigorously linear and monodirectional hypothesis of progress.

© Springer Nature Switzerland AG 2020
K. Hoshi and J. Waterworth, *Primitive Interaction Design*, Human–Computer Interaction Series,
https://doi.org/10.1007/978-3-030-42954-6_2

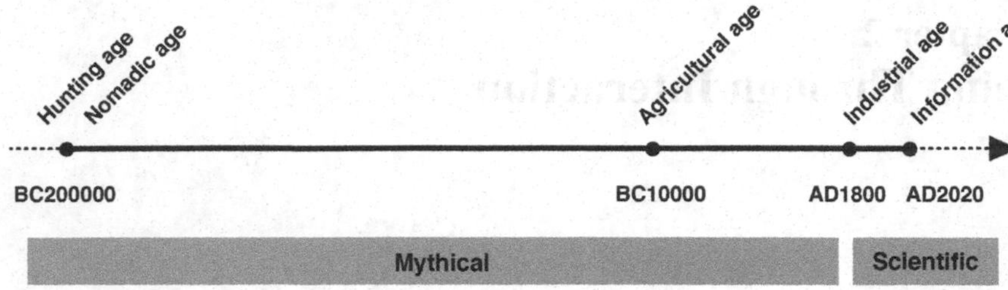

Fig. 2.1 History as linear progression

However, something radically different has happened because of the development of particular classes of information technology, something which gave us the opportunity to return to something like a pre-technological state of being. The context for these developments includes the increased frequency of our functioning in apparently three-dimensional (3D) virtual worlds, the linking of ubiquitous computers in a world-wide communication network and in large-scale social networks implemented on that base structure, along with a gradual breakdown in top-down control of the media.

2.1.1 Towards the Tangible

For many years now, almost everyone with complex data to explore has used three-dimensional representations to provide alternative ways of perceiving possible relationships in that data. This development was a major change in how specialists work, in their cognitive strategies and behaviours, since they have traditionally relied on their own skills of mental visualization and imagination to perceive such relationships. Internal mental visualization, problem-solving and imagination of possible structures are to a large extent being replaced by computer visualization, as well as other ways of rendering abstract information in concrete, tangible forms. These forms are not static but dynamic and the specialist can interact with the data in many ways, choose the viewpoint and manipulate how aspects of the data are presented. Investment advisors, surgeons, engineers, industrial designers, meteorologists, geologists, crystallographers and molecular biologists, amongst many others, use 3D computer graphics, and sometimes sounds and tactile displays, to experience information in ways that would have been impossible, or required tremendous imaginative efforts, to realize previously.

As more elements are visualized, aurelized and in other ways converted to concrete representations that can be directly apprehended by the human perceptual system, information is made real (occupying perceptible external space) by computer technology. In other words, the existence of interactive multi-modal computer-based realizations removes the need for much cognitive effort to be spent on realizing information mentally in imagination (as images). In this sense, specialists' experiences of information and their interactive behaviours in relation to it have become more primitive—more like the way a primitive person would deal with the physical world. Of course, the specialist can interactive with multiple realizations of the same information, whereas the physical world of the primitive is singular. But both realizations—3D computer graphics and the physical world—are tangible, interactive and directly shareable with others.

Many specialists believe that they can make more sense of information as a result, reflecting the view that to make sense means to make it into a form that can be experienced by the senses, and in this task the computer is more powerful than human imagination. Sense is not made until a concrete representation is experienced in human consciousness but, as human consciousness is very limited, effort spent on the process of imagining and holding the information necessary for concrete mental representations is effort that is not available to reflect on those representations. The positive side of this development is that transferring the task of realization to the computer frees conscious resources for other things, such as the problem analysis and hypothesizing of the specialist. And, of course, designers increasingly use 3D environments in their daily work. For the designer, 3D tools potentially provide a way of returning to a craft-like working process. This corresponds to a greater potential emphasis on mental being rather than mental doing or, put another way, physically doing what once required significant mental effort.

As an approach to interaction, tangible interfaces have a history dating back at least 30 years. Dourish (2001) is probably the best known HCI theorist to emphasize the coming shift towards the tangible. Many authors have written of the need to design for embodiment (e.g. Marshall and Hornecker 2013). With tangible user interfaces (TUIs), control is coupled with the model of the domain, not separate from it as it is in traditional models such as the Model–View–Controller (MVC). Hornecker and Buur (2006) had earlier argued that because TUIs include spatial interaction designers need to shift from the cognitive issues involved in designing GUIs to the phenomenological issues of designing the whole interaction.

Here, we are attempting to set this well-recognized trend within a broader perspective, one that emphasizes embodiment not only as a factor in HCI design, but rather claims that to do HCI design will increasingly be to design embodiment itself, to design our very being. This return to being as a focus of design can be seen as a threat or an opportunity. It is an opportunity to learn more about design in relation to conscious (and not so conscious) experience. On the other hand, a return to pre-technology, even a temporary, reversible one, is also a return to primitive ways of being and doing. And it is not clear that on the social level this "prehumanising" effect really is reversible. A turn or return to and of the primitive may be inevitable. And our modern psychology is not that of the primitive, as is clear when we compare current attitudes and experiences of time—our time, time passing, time as money, time as an absolute—with earlier views.

2.1.2 The Interactive Experience of Time

One of the key indicators of change in perspective and state of mind is the way the passage of time is experienced. It is a corollary of our state of being. This is because time is a primary dimension of human experience, temporality the essence of human mortality. But it is not something we perceive, but rather live in and through. We do not make machines to capture or collect time, but to define it. But that definition is not how we experience time, nor can it be.

People have reflected on the nature of time throughout history, observing changes in time in the world around them, and different changes in the experience of time in the world within them. Universally, exceptional and significant events are characterized by an alteration in the apparent flow of time. In "normal", everyday, working life time may seem to flow more or less regularly, but in dreams, in celebration, in moments of inspiration, in danger, in sickness and pain, in ecstasy and religious revelation, time does funny things. The nature of human experience would be profoundly different if it did not. Time can fly or it can drag, time stands still and time runs away from us. Time may be on our side or it may be against us, until the day our time runs out and we escape its clutches.

Time is intrinsic to shared meaning. We weave patterns in time to communicate our thoughts and feelings, in speech and music, in gestures, dance and song, in making love, and in silence. Social meanings rest on the assumption of a shared definition of the way in which time passes. Modern social interaction has increasingly emphasized adherence to time defined by standardized clocks. This can be seen as an external limitation on individual behaviour, and as such limitations increase in rigour the scope for variations in experience might be expected to be reduced.

We are frequently surprised by how quickly, or slowly, time has passed after engaging in a particular activity, despite years of experience of the way our perception of time can vary. But a serious inability to judge time, and particularly order, consistently is a feature of many psychiatric disorder states (Orme 1969). Yet, we often seek to alter our perception of time. We engage in activities to pass the time, to prevent its hanging heavily on our hands. Substances with the power to change time for us have been in demand throughout the ages and in virtually all cultures, and many religions have espoused techniques such as meditation and fasting, which also allow one to transcend the flow of conventionally defined time. Time, then, is important to us, and could be said to be central to our psychic life. As Sherover (1975) pointed out, "*if human experience is seen in any sense as bearing meaning and truth, then experiential time becomes crucial*".

The way in which time has been conceptualized has changed through history and from culture to culture, although certain themes recur. These "archetypal" views of the nature of time are reflected in the social conception of temporal behaviour and hence in the individual's experience of time. The conceptualisation of time has, for example, been related to individuals' philosophical orientations (Grunbaum 1963). Some societies have integrated the potential for escape from a rigidly defined conception of time into the fabric of daily life, as, for example, in the "Dream Theory" of the Senoi of Malaysia (Stewart 1972). In other societies, temporal arrangements have a fluid aspect, as when the basic temporal unit is the time taken to boil rice, or to walk to the next village. The social demands of "developed" communities have generally allowed for rather less variability. In rural societies, the most significant cyclic periods are those of the seasons, punctuated by four great annual festivals, whereas in urban living a weekly cycle predominates, marked by the relaxation of the weekend. Rural man is tied to the land, to plants, animals and the weather, which are locked into yearly cycles.

Modern man distanced himself from this but is just as rigidly tied by temporal constraints on behaviour through fairly arbitrarily defined time units. The existence of mechanical clocks, all ticking away practically indefinitely and in approximate agreement, has surely strengthened the belief in a uniform, continuous time. The power of the clock is demonstrated in those experiments that have used clock rate as an independent variable. Craik and Sarbin (1963), for example, found that covert changes in the rate at which a clock marked time passed unnoticed by most subjects, despite significant changes in rate of performance. Subjects trusted the clock more than any internal indicators of elapsed time. As one subject reported "*I was using my heartbeats (as cues) but it didn't work after a while, so I didn't believe them anymore*" (p. 607). In a similar study, McGrath and O'Hanlon (1970) report that subjects who served in conditions in which the clock rate was surreptitiously altered "*readily admitted to being fooled completely and accepted the displayed time as correct*" (p. 417). Both studies involved conditions where gross alterations were made to the clock (from half to double normal rate).

Technological development has, until recently, tended to increase the need for the accurate timing of human responses, but the impact of this on the development of consistent temporal perception has perhaps been mitigated by an increasing reliance on external timekeepers. Clocks are everywhere: in our workplaces, in our homes and cars, on our wrists, on our phones, computers and other interactive devices. While this frequent exposure to clocks has resulted in a fairly well-developed ability to judge the clock duration of intervals spent in familiar activities, our experience of time is nevertheless rather imperfectly mapped onto the social definition of time. Should we include clock-defined time in our designs, or should time be a dimension *of* design?. Subjective time is increasingly interactive time, since our interactive devices define time for us—and are designed to do that. But interactive time need not be clock-defined time.

We can see a potential for a return to a different way of experiencing time, an earlier way. Our problem, as citizens and designers, is that while we interact, via technology, in an increasingly primitive way, time is still defined for us by machines, rather than our changing nature. And yet, some developments support more subjective approaches to behaviour in time. TV and video on demand, combined with mobile communications, have removed the need to be in a particular place at a particular time when consuming media. In fact, we can design how users experience time—but this is not something that is part of contemporary design approaches.

Most modern designers have actually become slaves to clock-defined time in their work. To get back to being and the primacy of human experience (not machine-defined experience), designers need to break free from considerations of efficiency and time management, and move towards intimate and tangible interaction with the felt world. Emerging technologies can help them to do this. It a natural and necessary part of a return to being, not just in products, but also in the activities and experience of production. To escape from this, we introduce the idea of time flowing not linearly, but in a circle.

2.2 A Circular History of Being (and Interacting)

What is the purpose of realizing information? With the specialist, this is relatively easy to see. It is to find relationships that would otherwise have been missed, and whose perception would have required enormous mental effort. It is relatively easy to design tools in ways that support the work of specified types of specialist user (e.g. Mannapperuma et al. 2019).

How information is realized depends in such cases on the purpose of its realization, but in many others, and increasingly, there may be no clear purpose or one that can only be specified at a very high level (to have good experiences, to be quick, to avoid mental effort, to have fun). The criteria for the choices that characterize design are not obvious. However, with purpose or without, this process towards computer-based realizations seems to be inevitable and may be irreversible. We cannot avoid direct engagement with such information now that it is available and now that dealing with it is so central to our lives, because external reality is so seductive. Our senses are drawn to the primitive, and that is where we increasingly find meaning.

If, instead of our conventional linear view, we adopt a circular conception of history closer to some Eastern philosophies, we can understand this process. The point of arrival could also be the point of departure (Fig. 2.2). Having gone through science, we find ourselves returning to a more mythical and primitive stage. In our

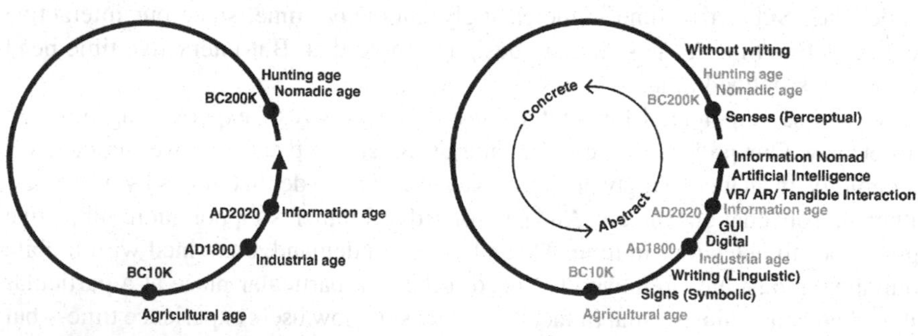

Fig. 2.2 Circular view of history and the way we interact(ed)

current era, which is characterized by more and more pervasive information in society, the perception of the "untamed mind" is ever more important. How we interact now, with virtual reality, movies, images and tweets instead of texts, is indicative of this return to being, to the concrete—and of the need for appropriately primitive ways of designing.

We can identify four main stage points in this circular journey through time. First, preliterate humans—humans before they really were human, but also the idealized primitive people—were in many ways much like any other animal. They responded to the immediate situation according to perceptions of the current situation. Their responses tended to be automatic—instinctive—and unreflective. In other words, cognition was largely unconscious. They did a lot of work with their legs and hands and almost none of this work needed much consciousness. But they were conscious. They experienced pleasure and pain, comfort and discomfort, hunger and fullness. And at some point in human development, they started to do more work, consciously. They started to plan their day to maximize success in hunting and minimize tiredness. They began to work out how to avoid dangers before encountering them.

In the second stage, the development of language co-occurred with, and enabled, increased cooperation between early people in activities such as food collection and hunting, shelter construction, childcare and so on. This also required an increase in abstract reasoning, an increase in conscious doing accompanied by a decrease in conscious being. Innocent being-in-the-world, which is still the state of the vast majority (possible all) of other animals, was lost in the process of acquiring language, and mankind started down a long path of abstract thinking, leading to the knowledge gained through philosophy, the sciences, maths and logic. At the same time, concrete reasoning still went on, in the arts, drama and sports, but already the two strands of human psychology and activity were separated and tended to be emphasized in different individuals.

The third stage represents a period when the pinnacle achievements of mankind became associated with conscious doing—abstract thought—rather than the products of contemplative being. At its height, this was reflected in a scientific optimism that all things would eventually be understood through the pursuit of science based on rational thought. The Arts (and design) became personal statements by individuals and largely peripheral to the thrust of modernity. God was declared dead and religion relegated to one day a week, at best. The separation of our minds from our bodies, our reason from our emotions, was complete. But at some point, perhaps as a result of world wars whose horror was largely identified with technological developments (such as weapons of global destructive capacity), people lost their optimism and enthusiasm for the products of conscious doing. The time was ripe for attempts to recombine being and doing, minds and bodies, rationality and feeling.

In the fourth stage, computer technology and associated communication capabilities were created—largely a result of efforts to win wars. However, and surprisingly, this most technological and abstract of inventions also came to provide the means for a reintegration of being and doing. Virtual Reality, through its creation of a concrete world from abstract data, opened up the possibility of man recovering his being while not forfeiting technological progress. This is technologically enhanced, post-literate man, in the situation where computer systems do the work of abstraction, and leave him free to contemplate and manipulate the concrete results.

Rose (2003) commented as follows: "Modern technologies—photography, film, video and audiotape, and above all the computer—restructure consciousness and memory even more profoundly [than the introduction of printing], imposing new orders upon our understanding of and actions upon the world". Rose sees this as a step further than printing, which stabilized uncertain observations into "facts". We are claiming that while this was true up to some point of history, the development of virtual realities and other interactive technologies effectively led us back beyond pre-printing, to preliterate modes of being. This casts design in a different light than that of the handmaid of linear development and progress.

Our consciousness and ways of working and being are reverting to an earlier state, a state in some ways of innocence, where consciousness is concerned with being rather than the mental doing—the hard conscious work of making concrete sense of abstract information—that has been a dominant feature of mental life since language first emerged. This is also not to say that we are all in some contemplative or meditational state—far from it. On the contrary, we are increasingly acting directly and immediately—in the present moment—through technology, often with little or no thought. We are becoming more primitive,

How do we design for this time of reversion to the concrete, the tangible and immediate, the primitive?

2.3 Being Through Interaction

To *be* with or through technology means to have the experience of unmediated interaction, as if with the physical world, even though one's engagement is with a technology-mediated reality. It is to have direct engagement that requires little or no thought about *how* to act, because actions are natural and intuitive. A well-designed technology-mediated world is one in which one feels present, in the here and now (Waterworth and Hoshi 2016).

The first step towards this direct kind of direct engagement and presence in a computer-mediated world was direct manipulation of "metaphorical" objects on the computer screen. Although not obvious at its inception, we can see now that a change from an abstract, language-based way of interacting with computers to one where computer entities (such as files) and processes (such as delete) are shown as directly manipulable objects (file icons and trash cans) was the first step in a profound shift towards concretising the abstract by computer, rather than by conscious effort.

Figure 2.3, based on the model of Waterworth and Chignell (1991), shows how these changes impact on our interactive behaviour, which leads directly to—and must be supported by—new ways of designing: more tangible, more immediate, more concrete and more like using objects in the physical world.

The high–low specificity axis refers to how clear the explorer is about what is being sought—a specific information query versus browsing around. This corresponds to

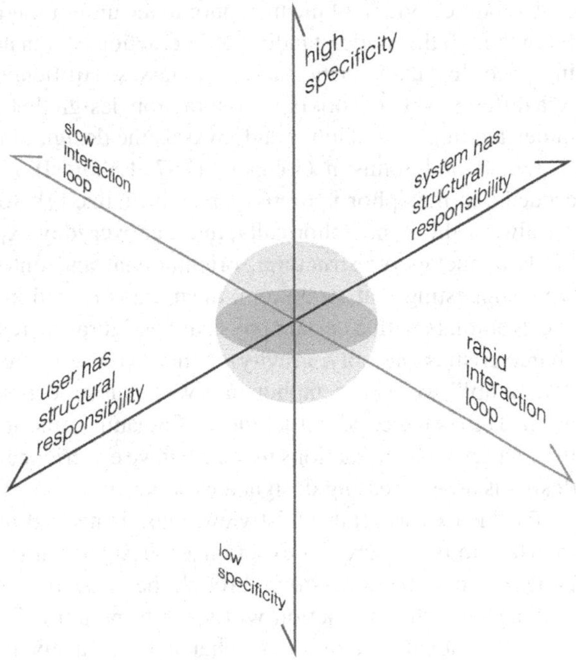

Fig. 2.3 Dimensions of interactive behaviour

the high–low focus dimension of mind presented in Fig. 2.4. The system-user responsibility axis refers to whether the system or the user does the searching (and must therefore be aware of the information terrain). This corresponds to the conscious–unconscious dimension of mind presented in Fig. 2.4. The rapid–slow interaction loop refers to the style of interacting with the information system. Rapid loops typify interactions based around direct manipulation and the manual following of links by the user. Slow loops arise when the user adopts a conversational style, perhaps describing a complete information request to an automated agent that will return with a response some time later. This corresponds to the frequent–infrequent sampling dimension of mind presented in Fig. 2.4.

The problem of interaction design has often been characterized as one of communication between the designer and the users of the interactive artefact. Norman's (1986) well-known account of interaction design centres on three kinds of model: the design model (in the head of the designer), the user's model (in the head of the user) and the system image (as presented in the designed interface). The system image serves as the medium of communication between the designer and the user. In the ideal case, the user's model comes to match the design model closely.

The common design approach to facilitating this process has been to incorporate one or more metaphors in the system image. It then becomes of great importance that the designer chooses appropriate metaphors which convey relevant aspects of the functionality of the system in terms that are understandable to the user. A good metaphor is a rhetorical device that is supposed to permit the user to apply knowledge of the source domain of the metaphor to the unfamiliar target domain of the interface. Even though this understanding of interaction design as the creation of metaphorical interfaces has many critics and weaknesses (Hurtienne 2017), it contains the germs of a different way of looking at interaction design that goes beyond the conventional understanding of metaphor and towards the design of embodiment.

Lakoff and Johnson (Johnson 1987; Lakoff 1987; Lakoff and Johnson 1980) argued that metaphor is more than a specialized rhetorical device. They argue that we always think metaphorically, that our everyday experiences are shaped by three kinds of metaphor: structural, orientational and ontological. Lakoff and Johnson were suggesting that, at bottom, meaning is rooted in basic, bodily, experiences of life as animals with a certain physical configuration residing on a planet with certain characteristics (notably, gravity). When we use expressions like, "I fell asleep" or "Wake up!" we use metaphor in a way that reflects the physical nature of life on earth. This is the experiential view of meaning, and it can be applied to understand interaction. Our interactions mean what we experience them to mean, and interaction design is about creating designed experiences.

By this experiential realist view, what is needed in interaction design is for the interface to be a source of experiences, designed in such a way that the experiences generated may be understood through the projection of image schemata. When this is done well, the interaction will seem to be unmediated by the technology. What the resultant interface means, what it is for a given user, depends on his or her unconscious reactions to the structures provided. If the interface feels right and works for its purpose with minimal reflection—in the same way the body works—it is successful. No designer can know what a technology really is. It is what it means to individual users and, like life or poetry, it means what it is experienced to be. Several recent technologies make this clearer.

In several recent publications, Turner and associates (Turner et al. 2014; Turner 2016) have put forward the idea that often interfaces are metaphorical but that we pretend that they are real. They suggest that, since metaphor clearly involves imagination, imagination is needed to make sense of interactions. We make-believe they are real and thus imagine their meaning. But when we feel truly present, when we interact in a primitive way—say when shooting a simulated enemy with a digital gun—we do not need to make-believe, pretend or use our imaginations (to make it real). For us, like the physical world often is, it *is* real. And yet, it also has a metaphorical aspect, along the lines of Lakoff and Johnson's cognitive realism. In this sense, metaphor does not imply the use of imagination. Rather, imagination implies the use of metaphor!

We can only understand the world and its possibilities through our bodies, and from the metaphorical projections of embodied image schemata that give it meaning and make imagination possible. Not only does our body structure meaning. In its relation to the spatial world around it, it also provides an anchor for mental activity. This is how, by interacting with designed technology, we can carry out meaningful activities via bodily actions. The relationship between mind, body and world is mutual and circular.

We habitually and naturally locate our thoughts and plans in space and in this way reduce the burden on our very limited consciousness. Our cognition is distributed (see Hutchins 2001, for an overview of work in the area). When we forget something, we can often retrieve the memory by revisiting the location, acting out the same physical movements, in which we first had the thought. This principle, acted out in the imagination, has served as the basis for many mnemonic systems through history (Yates 1966). Virtually spatial interfaces to information systems serve as artificial memory for their users, in the same way that physical spaces such as offices do. Because such systems are artificial but not merely imaginary, they can capitalize on both imagery and spatial memory in the recollection of the location of items of information.

2.3.1 Interaction, the Conscious and the Unconscious

Figure 2.4 represents an attempt to identify the main dimensions of mind. The high–low focus axis refers to the extent to which our attention is directed to fine-grain detail or the broad stroke features of a situation. This may be our sampling of the environment or our conscious processing of previously sampled information. The conscious–unconscious axis refers to how conscious we are. This is often correlated with level of "wakefulness" although we may actually be largely unconscious while

Fig. 2.4 Dimensions of mind and of (inter)action

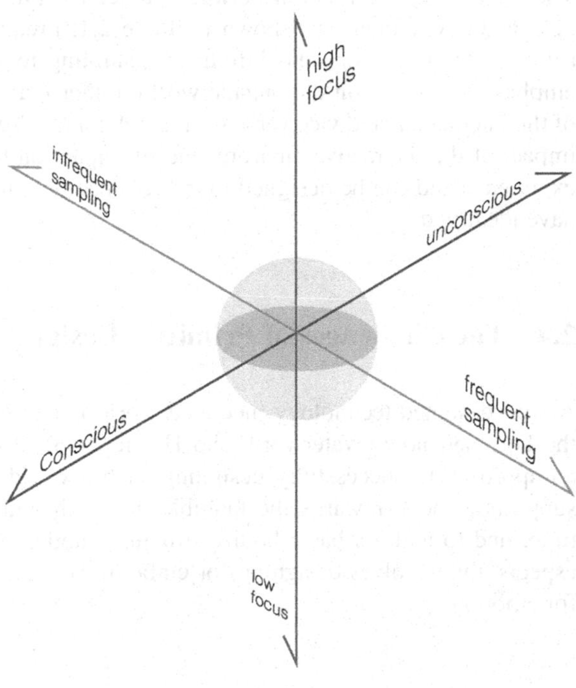

Table 2.1 Being-in-the-world: presence and time perception

	Mental being	Mental doing
Frequent sampling	Watching the sunset (High presence/slow time)	Daydreaming (Low presence/slow time)
Infrequent sampling	Climbing a difficult rock face (High presence/fast time)	Solving a logical puzzle (Low presence/fast time)

awake and highly conscious when asleep (as in vivid dreaming). The frequent–infrequent sampling axis refers to how frequently the individual samples from the stimuli received by the senses (as illustrated in Fig. 2.4). Rapid sampling will tend to occur when the conscious processing load is light and will be accompanied by the experience of time passing relatively slowly.

There is a natural correspondence between the dimensions of mind and those of interactive behaviour. Consciousness gives information meaning, through reflected bodily experiences. This way of looking at consciousness and its relationship to computer systems also gives us a possible approach to deliberately design for creativity. Often, creativity is seen as mysterious or even mystical. One reason for this is that new ideas seem to enter consciousness almost spontaneously, presumably from the unconscious. The correspondence of the conscious–unconscious dimension with the structural responsibility dimension (see Fig. 2.3) underlines this state of affairs.

Taking these models of mind and the design dimensions of interaction, we can also expand on the relation between subjective time and sense of presence in a designed environment, as shown in Table 2.1. Frequent sampling corresponds to a fast interaction loop, and infrequent sampling to a slower pace. Mental being emphasizes a focus on the outside world, rather than on the internal mental world of the interactant, and vice versa for mental doing. The form, content and emotional impact of the interactive environment all impact on the nature of the interactant's experience and can be designed to induce specific effects along the dimensions we have identified.

2.4 The Challenges of Primitive Design

A well-designed technology-mediated world is one in which one feels present, in the here and now (Waterworth and Hoshi 2016). Primitive Interaction Design is an approach to successfully designing such a world. Primitive interaction design supports a move towards the tangible, to mesh with the personal experience of time, and to address basic bodily structures underlying meaning. Amongst other aspects, this involves designing for embodiment and—integral to that—designing for emotion.

2.4.1 Designing for Emotion

Emotions can be understood as reactions to situations in which an organism finds itself, as part of our evolved response systems affecting both the body and the mind. Emotions such as the discomfort arising from pain help an organism to avoid damage and increase the chances of survival. When emotions tend to persist or recur over longer periods—of hours and days rather than seconds—they are sometimes called moods. Here, we use the term "emotion" rather loosely, to cover both these types of affective response. In this sense, emotion is now well accepted as an important ingredient of successful human–computer interaction (HCI) design. It has arguably always been important in design (for what else distinguishes two equally functional and cost-effective designs?), but as a discipline rooted in the methods and mindset of the cognitive psychology of the 70s and 80s, HCI was slow to accept that affect is as important as mental problem-solving—or rather, that emotion and logical problem-solving work together in almost all our practical reasoning about the world around us (e.g. Damasio 1994, 1999).

In the design of HCI, both software and hardware, it is important to keep in mind that not all emotions are equal. As an evolved response system aimed at survival, negative feedback in the form of unpleasant emotional experiences is particularly important. Why? Because, when things are going well, no state-changing response is needed—as with any homeostatic control system. When we are in danger, or hungry, or sexually frustrated, we experience emotions so that and as we respond to make necessary changes to our situation. The "motion" in emotion gets us out of a bad place and into a potentially better one. Arguably, positive emotions are what we feel when things are going fine, when we don't feel negative emotions. Feeling good does not help us meet challenges; at best it helps us stay put, in a good place. But emotions are not only triggered by the situations we encounter. We can feel emotions just as strongly in imagined or recalled situations as in the present reality, and in response to events we know to be fictional in, say, a film or a novel (Russell 2003). It follows that any successful and advanced organism must be able to answer the following questions (though not necessarily in this order):

- Is this happening in the world around me, or only in my head?
  (answered on the basis of whether I feel present in an external environment)
- Is this likely to be true or is it fiction?
  (answered on the basis of a reality judgment)
- Do I need to avoid this, and how urgently?
  (answered on the basis of an emotional experience)

The sense of presence allows us to assess whether a designed experience is happening in the world around us or is a construction created in internal mental space (Waterworth et al. 2015). For example, first-person video games usually try to convey the impression that one is physically located in the portrayed scenes, often with others. In contrast, a well-constructed novel may produce equally vivid experiences, but these are felt to exist in the mind of the reader, not in the world around him, and so are not directly shareable. This distinction of feeling the location of an experience reveals the presence mechanism in action.

Overall presence level depends on how well integrated the cognitive system is to focus on the environment around the individual. Emotion can affect this in several different ways, affecting the top and bottom layers. For example, by creating an arousing effect that orientates the individual to attend to the environment (stimulating presence) from the bottom up, presence will be increased. On the other hand, emotion induced at higher levels may increase attention to the environment or reduce it, depending on whether the content is associated with the current environment (presence) or independent of it.

The extent to which mediated experiences evoke a strong feeling of presence, of being bodily situated in a portrayed, surrounding world, changes over time, through the development of changing personal and cultural *media schemata* (Ijsselsteijn 2005). When the first jumpy, grainy, black and white movies were shown to audiences, the impact was extraordinary: scenes of an approaching train caused members of the audience to run out of the cinema in panic. Today, even wide screens, surround-sound systems and vibrating cinema seats cannot evoke such a dramatic response, although imperfections in the integration of information supplied to the different senses may result in nausea, eyestrain, headaches or other negative systems of "cybersickness". Within individuals, media schemata seem to adjust themselves in the light of experience: cinematic special effects that were breathtakingly impressive in the early 1980s will have relatively little impact on the same viewer 20 years later.

There is also evidence that as our experience of apparently realistic media increases, some of our responses to our evolved psychological mechanisms are being modified. So-called "inverse presence" (Timmins and Lombard 2005) refers to the phenomenon, whereby real events are experienced as computer-mediated. This occurred, for example, when observers saw camera footage of the World Trade Centre tragedy in New York, which many viewers judged to be the result of digital special effects. And in the "uncanny valley" effect, first suggested by Mori in 1970 (Mori 2012), although robots generally increase in judged pleasantness as their apparent humanness increases, a point is reached where the robot becomes so very nearly realistic that observers find it repulsive. A similar effect may result from interactive experiences of very high apparent realism, especially those involving human-like avatars.

Within a given time and culture, individual people also vary in their preference and capacity for presence. Since presence is, for us, a reflection of the extent to which an individual is engaged with (and feels able to act in) an external world rather than with an internal world of the imagination, we would expect personality factors that are well known to affect this relation (Eysenck 1997) to also affect experienced presence. For example, we might expect that extrovert personalities in general prefer higher presence than introvert personalities. Similarly, elderly people might be expected to prefer less presence in interactive situations than the young (Waterworth et al. 2018).

An important implication of these differences is that the same interactive environment will have differing impacts on different individuals, and should be designed either with the user's presence preferences in mind, or in a way that adapts to this. Since it is often difficult or impossible to assess personality and other individual characteristics in advance, the best way to address this is to be sensitive to the participant's changing state during the interaction. This sensitivity of the system to the individual can take the form of bio- or psycho-feedback, and thus the approach to individuals can actually be generalizable across individuals.

2.4.2 Designing Embodiment

To practice primitive design is to create a sense of presence in a seemingly concrete world. This sense of presence in a computer-mediated design environment is a function of the possibilities for direct action in that space, in the same way that feeling present in the physical world is grounded in perception and bodily action. Unless we can act directly in the world, we will not feel ourselves to be greatly present in it. When we act in mediated worlds, we may interact through different degrees and forms of embodiment and this has implications for the extent to which we potentially can feel present in the world (Haans and IJsselsteijn 2012).

There are at least three ways in which technology can impact our sense of being embodied: through expanded, altered and distributed embodiment. 'Expanded embodiment' is part and parcel of mediated presence as the term is commonly understood (Bracken and Skalski 2010). This is most clear in a VR environment where the actual physical surroundings are shielded from the user as far as possible—to avoid distraction away from the virtual world. These distractions have been termed "breaks in presence" (Slater and Steed 2000) but are actually shifts of presence from the virtual world to in the physical world. Our embodiment is released from the envelope of the physical body. The design challenges here are as limitless as the possibilities.

Whenever computer-based information is blended with the perception of the surrounding physical world, as in augmented reality, this may become integrated into a new form of altered embodiment. But that requires that the augmentation of the physical with the virtual be designed in such a way that the user has the potential to feel present. Given the clear popularity of mobility and social connectivity, it seems that presence will increasingly be experienced through attention to an external world in which the physical and the virtual are somehow blended. For this to work in practice, a major challenge is to make media devices sensitive to the situational context of their use, and the state of their users. Presence levels could in principle then be dynamically adjustable to maintain optimal functioning in an unfolding blended reality stream. If this can be achieved, then true Ambient Intelligence might become a reality irrespective of personal location. The design space of sensory transformations with technology is also huge, which provides enormous potential but is also highly challenging for designers. We can see that 'altered embodiment' opens up a new way of being in a world, and of experiencing presence. Indeed, it changes not only the body but also the perceived form of the physical world in which the body is located. In designing altered embodiment, the possibilities are almost endless—but we do not yet know much about what will work best for which purpose, or about possible longer term effects on the perceiver.

'Distributed embodiment' goes beyond these examples, by separating the observer from the observed body. There is an interesting parallel with the idea of embodied cognition. As mentioned earlier, our mental life relies on the use of external objects, events and their mutual configuration to hold ideas and memories. In some sense, our cognition is located in the objects around us. Distributed embodiment means that our bodies are, to some degree, located in the bodies around us. It is experientially very similar to naturally occurring out-of-the-body experiences (Blackmore 1984). As Petkova and Ehrsson (2008) report:

> Manipulation of the visual perspective, in combination with the receipt of correlated multisensory information from the body was sufficient to trigger the illusion that another person's body or an artificial body was one's own. This effect was so strong that people could experience being in another person's body when facing their own body and shaking hands with it. (Petkova and Ehrsson 2008, from the abstract)

Design challenges of distributed embodiment include specifying the means of being in other bodies, of switching between bodies and the characteristics of those bodies—which could include human (self or not, lifelike or not), robotic, animal (Nagel 1974) or even inanimate objects (Misselhorn 2009). It is likely that not all these possibilities will be effective in practice.

2.5 Conclusions

In this chapter, we have examined the way we interact(ed) based on a circular view of the history of being. What was once thought about in an abstract way can now be experienced directly, through direct experience, physical action and associated emotions. This brings a profound change to our perception and emphasizes that, however useful it may have been for solving practical problems, mental life also has the primary purpose of experience, of imparting a sense of being.

We are rediscovering that the mind is not an abstract, computational machine, which just happens to be conscious. We are emerging from an epoch where abstract reasoning was seen as the high point of human existence, and entering a new age of self-discovery (or self-destruction) made possible by the development of interactive technologies. In these environments, we experiment with what it means to be, not only with what it is possible to do.

With recent interactive technologies, we make tangible the intangible, "concretize" the abstract. This means that what was once thought about in an abstract way can now be experienced directly, through direct experience, physical action and associated emotions. We are returning to a more primitive state of being, and we need a more primitive way of designing based on relevant insights that encompass tangible experiences, subjective duration and emotional involvement in interaction.

Primitive interaction design is centrally concerned with our embodiment. Through advances in technology, it takes us from designing simple tools to match our bodies, to designing our very embodiment. And addressing the latter need, it also creates, according to our circular view of time, the possibility to develop direct, tangible design tools to use in the new realities in which we experience embodiment.

In the next chapter, we start to sketch the way forward by moving from current design thinking to a more mythical thinking style that lies at the core of Primitive Interaction Design. We then attempt to identify common attributes—or primitives—of ways of thinking and design in relation to untamed/savage/mythical minds. We discuss the significance of the untamed mind as applied to design thinking and show how designers with untamed minds can be advocates for alternative design mindsets in the years to come.

References

Blackmore S (1984) A psychological theory of the out-of-body experience. J Parapsychol 48:201–218

Bracken C, Skalski P (eds) (2010) Immersed in media: telepresence in everyday life. Routledge, New York

Craik KH, Sarbin TR (1963) Effect of covert alterations of clock rate upon time estimations and personal tempo. Percept Mot Skills 16:597–610

Damasio A (1994) Decartes' error: emotion, reason and the human brain. Penguin Putnam, New York, USA

Damasio A (1999) The feeling of what happens: body, emotion and the making of consciousness. Harcourt Brace and Co Inc., San Diego, CA

Dourish P (2001) Where the action is: the foundations of embodied interaction. MIT Press, Cambridge, MA

Eysenck HJ (1997) Personality and experimental psychology: the unification of psychology and the possibility of a paradigm. J Pers Soc Psychol 73(6):1224–1237

Grunbaum A (1963) Philosophical problems of time and space. Knopf

Haans A, IJsselsteijn WA (2012) Embodiment and telepresence: toward a comprehensive theoretical framework. Interact Comput 24(4):211–218. https://doi.org/10.1016/j.intcom.2012.04.010.

Hornecker E, Buur J (2006) Getting a grip on tangible interaction: a framework on physical space and social interaction. In: Proceedings of the SIGCHI conference on human factors in computing systems (CHI '06). Association for Computing Machinery, New York, NY, USA, pp 437–446. https://doi.org/10.1145/1124772.1124838

Hurtienne J (2017) How cognitive linguistics inspires HCI: image schemas and image-schematic metaphors. Int J Hum Comput Interact 33(1):1–20. https://doi.org/10.1080/10447318.2016.1232227

Hutchins E (2001) Distributed cognition. In: Smelser NJ, Baltes PB (eds) International encyclopedia of the social & behavioral sciences. Pergamon Press. ISBN: 978-0-08-043076-8
IJsselsteijn WA (2005) Towards a neuropsychological basis of presence. Annu Rev Cyber Therapy Telemed 3:25–30
Johnson M (1987) The body in the mind: the bodily basis of meaning, imagination and reason. University of Chicago Press
Lakoff G (1987) Woman, fire and dangerous things: What categories reveal about the mind. The University of Chicago Press, Chicago
Lakoff G, Johnson M (1980) Metaphors we live by Chicago. The University of Chicago Press
Mannapperuma C, Street N, Waterworth J (2019) Designing usable bioinformatics tools for specialized users. In: Information technology and systems: proceedings of ICITS 2019. Springer , Cham, pp 649–670. https://doi.org/10.1007/978-3-030-11890-7_62
Marshall P, Hornecker E (2013) Theories of embodiment in HCI. In: Price S, Jewitt C, Brown B (eds) The SAGE handbook of digital technology research. https://dx.doi.org/10.4135/9781446282229.n11
McGrath JJ, O'Hanlon J (1970) Temporal orientation and vigilance performance. In: Sanders AF (ed) Attention and performance.
Misselhorn C (2009) Empathy with inanimate objects and the uncanny valley. Mind Mach 19:345. https://doi.org/10.1007/s11023-009-9158-2
Mori M (2012) The uncanny valley (trans by MacDorman KF, Kageki N). IEEE Robot Autom 19(2):98–100. https://doi.org/10.1109/MRA.2012.2192811
Nagel T (1974) What is it like to be a bat? Philos Rev 83(4):435–450
Norman DA (1986) User-centered system design: new perspectives on human-computer Interaction. In: Norman DA, Draper SW (eds) Cognitive engineering. Lawrence Erlbaum Associates, Hillsdale, pp 31–61
Orme JE (1969) Time, experience and behaviour. Iliffe, London
Petkova VI, Ehrsson HH (2008) If I were you: perceptual illusion of body swapping. PLoS ONE 3(12):e3832
Rose S (2003) The making of memory: from molecules to mind. Vintage, Harmondsworth
Russell JA (2003) Core affect and the psychological construction of emotion. Psychol Rev 110(1):145–172. https://doi.org/10.1037/0033-295x.110.1.145
Sherover CM (1975) The human experience of time. NYU Press, New York
Slater M, Steed AJ (2000) A virtual presence counter. Presence: Teleoper Virtual Environ 9(5):413–434
Stewart K (1972) In: Tart CT (ed) Altered states of consciousness. Anchor, New York
Timmins LR, Lombard M (2005) When "real" seems mediated: inverse presence. Presence: Teleoper Virtual Environ 14(4):492–500
Turner P (2016) Presence: is it just pretending? AI Soc 31:147–156. https://doi.org/10.1007/s00146-014-0579-y
Turner P, Turner S, Carruthers L (2014) It's not interaction, it's make believe. In: Proceedings of the 2014 European conference on cognitive ergonomics (ECCE '14). Association for Computing Machinery, New York, NY, USA, Article 22, pp 1–8. https://doi.org/10.1145/2637248.2637266
Waterworth JA, Chignell MH (1991) A model for information exploration. Hypermedia 3(1):35–58. https://doi.org/10.1080/09558543.1991.12031189
Waterworth J, Hoshi K (2016) Human-experiential design of presence in everyday blended reality: living in the here and now. Springer, Switzerland
Waterworth JA, Waterworth EL, Riva G, Mantovani F (2015) Presence: form, content and consciousness. In: Lombard M, Biocca F, Freeman J, IJsselsteijn W, Schaevitz RJ (eds) Immersed in media: telepresence theory, measurement & technology. Springer. ISBN: 978-3-319-10189-7

Waterworth JA, Chignell M, Moller H, Kandylis D (2018) Presence and human development: age-specific variations in presence and their implications for the design of life-enhancing interactive applications. In: Proceedings of PRESENCE 2018, 18th conference of the International Society for Presence Research (ISPR), Prague, May 21–22. ISBN: 978-0-9792217-6-7
Yates F (1966) The art of memory. University of Chicago Press, Chicago

Part II
Theories and Foundations

In Part II, we expand on the potential of drawing on what we call primitive interaction design through a consideration of the savage or untamed mind in the development of interactive systems for a range of application areas. We specifically argue for the importance of myth as a source of design creativity, and particularly the character Trickster as a designer role model—as a mediator between mythical and modern thought—an alternative for designers who have fallen under the spell of instrumental rationality.

Next, we explore the world of the senses from an experiential perspective, which has largely become a delusive world for science, suggesting that untamed minds are characterized by using more of their sensory perceptions to support certain mental capacities for observation that modern "tamed" people have lost. We relate this to the creation of interactive environments, especially emerging digital-physical blended spaces. This is an approach to designing spaces that resonates with the functional needs and minds of their users' activities by also maintaining a degree of emptiness, to be filled unconsciously with sensory aspects of experiences. We speculate that "Ma", the Japanese concept of space and emptiness, is an essential aspect of the successful design of such interactive environments. Further, we explore the possibilities for universal design via a view of the universality of mind in Zen philosophy and transpersonal psychology, emphasizing phenomenology and experiential ontology in terms of eight levels of consciousness.

Chapter 3
Savage and Trickster

> *The red rainbow across the sky was as the sky taking on colour. The white sunlight was the sky growing bright. Yet the empty sky, but its nature, was not something to become bright. It was not something to take on colour. With a spirit like the empty sky he gave colour to all the varied scenes, but not a trace remained.*
> Kawabata, Y. (1968). Nobel Lecture: Japan, the Beautiful and Myself. *Nobel Prize in Literature, 12.*

Abstract In this chapter, we explore the characteristic patterns of mythological thought and its universality, shared among all mankind, as a complement to the more detailed and logical thought of modern "civilized" society. We see both methods towards acquiring knowledge, scientific and mythical thought, as equally valid in design. They are two ways of thinking, rather than two stages in the evolution of thought. We then attempt to apply mythical thought as an alternative design approach to the ordinary interaction design mindset. We go on to examine the cultural role of Trickster, which in some ways can be seen as parallelling a potential cultural/social role of a designer. The designer seen as trickster offers such catalysts as raising awareness, creating optimal conditions for a cultural paradigm shift or even introducing a fundamental meta-narrative into a particular culture.

3.1 Introduction: Before and After Design

Consider the view that design is inertia stemming from repeated practice. For example, think of a sketch that is being repeatedly drawn to meet the changing needs of the market. This way of thinking posits that design will never propel history; that is to say, design is a part of the "primitive". This is the interpretation of design according to people who call out to move the world forward through scientific pursuits. According to these people, designers are essentially "primitive".

What is the true nature of this misunderstood inertia of design? What changes are needed in our thinking for design to break through this barrier of misunderstanding? Mythological thinking and Eastern philosophy provide specific hints for answering

© Springer Nature Switzerland AG 2020

K. Hoshi and J. Waterworth, *Primitive Interaction Design*,
Human–Computer Interaction Series,
https://doi.org/10.1007/978-3-030-42954-6_3

these questions. Both of them share a deeper understanding of human beings as a species on the subconscious level.

Designs that resonate throughout human society reflect universal principles shared across the globe. Such designs are shared in the human subconscious.

According to Jung (2014), systems of dreams and myths have commonalities. Both come from a profound part of the subconscious, which is shared across the human race. In this chapter, we will shed light on how our thinking of design and information-based society should adapt moving forward by using universal thinking and consciousness in coexistence with modern information technology.

3.2 The Logic of Myth

Lévi-Strauss (2013) claimed that myths were the first form of human philosophy. Philosophy considers the essence of human beings and is willing to overturn the rules in society for this purpose, and myths similarly explore a reversal of societal rules. In denying these rules, they consider what it means to be human on a more cosmic level. In this way, myths are the first form of human philosophy. *Why are we here?* This is the difficult riddle that confronts us. Myths are created to help us deal with the contradictions we face. Other animals do not have to consider such contradictions. It is only human beings who—through culture—have produced these irreconcilable contradictions. In other words, mythological thinking is a state of cognition that the world is made as a mass of contradictions.

Culture is created through the process of classification. This process results in the rejection of the totality of nature. This thereby creates a divide between culture and nature, marking a fundamental contradiction that has existed since *homo sapiens* first appeared on the earth. The divided world is structured in a state of opposition, such as with the rainy and dry seasons. Neither one can exist without the other, and the world falls into barrenness without either of them. To overcome this, the world accepts and incorporates these contradictions. Rain, as a negative force in nature, inundates itself on the fertile world repeatedly in order to perpetuate the cycle of life. Life in this world cannot persist abundantly with either nature or culture alone. The two must work in a mutual cycle in order to sustain the living world, and the universe can only persist through the repetition of this process of contradictions. Myths are a form of philosophy because—by allowing us to accept contradictions and divisions—they include philosophical thinking for creating a rich reintegration for the world. According to Levi-Strauss (1966), myths are based on analytical reasoning.

Design is a process that merges that which is difficult to externalize together with that which is easy to externalize, and does so in a fulfilling way. In other words, design is able to achieve an enriched world by reintegrating objective and subjective thinking—two divided and separated concepts. The designer cannot be considered "primitive"; nor can indigenous peoples be considered "primitive".

When using objective thought as a yardstick, the thoughts of designers and so-called "primitives" are considered to be undeveloped, as they do not order things through a logical process of categorization and resort to a wholly illogical "mystical participation" that mixes hierarchies and order without logic. Opinions from an objective standpoint view such people as if to be thoughtless, though such opinions are far removed from reality, and are rife with prejudice. On the contrary, the designer's thought works to destroy the externalized order of the objectivist and attempts to achieve integration with that which cannot be put into words.

3.3 "Primitive" Peoples

Anthropologists in the twentieth century were surprised to find that the primitive societies they researched had in fact observed the world around them in excruciating detail. These societies had specific knowledge on the natural objects and events surrounding them, and were able to skillfully take advantage of these in their daily lives. Logic is an inherent part of the senses, and this logic contains intelligence within it. Since our inception, human beings have always been intelligent beings, and our intelligence has manifested itself through the use of concrete objects. For example, so-called primitive societies use their sharpened intellect to precisely record highly minute changes in natural phenomena, such as the sense of belongingness among living creatures (both aquatic and terrestrial), as well as wind, light, the colour of the sky, and the size and type of ocean waves, air currents and water currents. Levi-Strauss (1966) referred to this form of intellect as the "science of the concrete".

This theory integrates the intellect with the senses, in which the five senses are used to make logical thinking. Rather than using abstract concepts to understand things like modern people, they used concrete things that were readily found in the natural and human world, fully utilizing their five senses in order to intelligently think about and understand the world. This is the essence of Lévi-Strauss's "science of the concrete".

In his writings, Levi-Strauss (1966) states that the people of the Neolithic era or from the beginning of history are the heirs to a long scientific tradition. In other words, the thinking approaches of so-called "primitive" people across the world are the same as the approaches of people in the Neolithic era. The thought of people from early history, from antiquity, and from medieval times has all similarly inherited this scientific thinking present since the Paleolithic era.

By the late Paleolithic era, the same *homo sapiens* as those alive today are believed to have recited poetry, told myths and performed rituals. Though it is also believed that these peoples were already engaged in primitive forms of scientific thinking, there are not sufficient historical records present. However, by the Neolithic era, the knowledge of the late Paleolithic era accumulated over some 30,000 years began to take a structure in a magnificent manner. Fragments of natural observations and mythological stories were systemized. Large-scale myths began to form, along with the establishment of defined rituals. The Neolithic era saw the emergence of technologies vital for civilization, including earthenware, weaving, farming and the domestication of animals. Nonetheless, the essential developments had already started in the late Paleolithic era (Colomina and Wigley 2016).

People in this time worked on the basis of thorough observations and used plants and animals for food and economic purposes. Not only that, they even thought about the plants and animals they did not utilize in their daily lives, along with natural phenomena related to wind and water—an intellect that Lévi-Strauss refers to as the "Savage Mind". This period marks the beginning of a body of knowledge based on classification and concrete replacements. Their efforts to satisfy their intellectual curiosity are just like those of a natural scientist.

In comparing their approach to modern scientists, Levi-Strauss (1966) uses the term "magical thinking", which posits that the intellectual processes used in science and magic are essentially the same. This term attempts to clarify the origin of modern science as a result of accumulated "magical" knowledge from the Neolithic era.

Scientific thinking is built on "concepts". Concepts are abstract and—as much as possible—omit specific conditional factors. They serve as intellectual tools to fit designated applications. The concepts utilized by scientists and engineers are applied in laboratory work, research and in the creation of new products. On the contrary, the thinking approach of "primitive" peoples is based on semiotics. In the same vein, magical practices also use signs for bricolage. Many of the practices born in the Neolithic age, such as magic, myths and rituals, are based on the system of bricolage. Though conceived in a different era and place, we use these practices in our thinking today. The concept of bricolage is discussed in detail in Chap. 6.

Is there really such a thing as "emptiness" or "gaps"? Did "primitive" people have the capability to perceive such concepts? "Emptiness" and "gaps" are perceived to be self-transforming properties, accompanied by bricolage across eras through conscious or unconscious processes. "Primitive" peoples certainly had the ability to recognize these concepts. In any era, the concept of "emptiness" and "gaps" lead any created object to seem incomplete. As such, people set off to build once more. With a new bricolage comes a new accompanying presence of "emptiness" and "gaps". This is what leads to the formation of a rich world of cultures. The concepts of "emptiness" and "gaps" are discussed in detail in Chap. 4.

Scientists invent concepts to deal with problems. These concepts are used to create an ordered world. On the other hand, the world created through bricolage is inevitably given mythological properties. This world shares commonalities and properties with self-transforming myths. Levi-Strauss (1966) stated that practitioners of magic and practitioners of science have the same essential psychological makeup. Magic and science later diverged into two different directions, whereby we consider scientific thinking to be correct and magical thinking to be incorrect or outdated in the present day. However, in A Savage Mind, Lévi-Strauss flatly denies such judgments. He claims that the tools and methods used by scientists today are entirely the result of methods that had already been devised through magical thinking.

The scientific world omits or denies the existence of that which cannot be expressed in words. Consider concepts such as "emptiness" and "gaps". Since these are outside of the realm of science, their existence is not discussed. Hereupon lies the reason for the incongruity of the magical with the scientific. As such the criterion for defining thought as either objective or subjective is whether or not that thought deals with "emptiness" or "gaps". As these concepts are utilized in daily life and in manufacturing, such practice is far removed from science. In this way, science has evolved denying the existence of "emptiness" and "gaps".

This is why design can never be considered a science. The objectivist posits that the non-scientific is subjective, that actions under such a premise merely derive from inertia and that practitioners of such actions are "primitive".

3.4 The Trickster

There is one character that perfectly embodies the role of the designer in mythology: the "trickster" (Levi-Strauss 1966; Yamaguchi 1993; Hosoe et al. 1991. The trickster surpasses time and space, and possesses commonalities seen throughout numerous myths across the world. He or she disturbs and destroys order, while also creating a new order. In mythology, the trickster plays the role of a mediator or arbitrator regarding fundamental conflicts.

This character is found throughout the world and possesses a role in sharp contrast with that of the "priest", whose duty is to ensure the stability of the system.

Jung (2014) suggests that archetypes reflect different aspects of human personality, and claims that our personalities are subdivided in order to act out the drama of human life. Jung noticed commonalities in his patients' dreams and myths, and claimed that these commonalities came from an area in the deep subconsciousness that runs common among all human beings. Myths, or stories based on their models, are commonly enjoyed among all people. This is because they are accepted by the common subconscious among human beings and run in line with universal principles that reflect a sense of perception seen in people around the world.

If the essence of the designer is to create things or concepts with a story to which anyone can relate, the designer's ideal way of being is to act or implement the thought of the trickster or the savage. This follows universal principles that reflect a shared global consciousness. To realize truly universal design, it is necessary to introduce designs that can be shared across the human subconscious and universally reflect a global shared consciousness.

The terms "fool", "clown" and "buffoon" are generally used in a derogatory way. To be a fool suggests that one is scatter-brained. To call someone a clown in a political context means that they are unreliable. Positivist rationalism limits itself to visible and quantitative reality. As a ritual framework for communication, the moral view in Western-European modern civic society discards all forms of expression except for that which can be externally considered to be "serious". This view only recognizes individual people as improving statistics, and in other words is of a world dominated by a sense of humanity that denies all variables. In such a world, it is only natural that the "fool", who makes a living by transforming without any awareness of his or her limits, would be made an outcast. The "fool" is only considered to be chaotic or confused because this world is unable to produce any words, logic or system that can express the nature of foolishness in a consistent manner.

The "fool" acts by breaking free from everyday logic. As such, there is no need for his or her actions to be restricted by the value systems of everyday life. In this sense, the "fool" is permitted to behave as freely as a child (Yamaguchi 1988). The "fool" reveals through this role that there is no basis or meaning in presumably "meaningful" actions carried out in daily life, and that things considered absolute are in fact relative.

The "fool" forgoes channels of communication established by objectivity or science, and forges a new, untapped path for communication. The "fool" plays a role of guiding us to an as-yet-unknown reality. If necessary, the "fool" will take us to irrational or absurd places. The "fool" merges the unknown with the everyday, functioning like a "priest" who is not sanctioned by society. One encounters the "fool" upon realizing that the edge of reason is simply the starting point for a more comprehensive point of reason. The "trickster" and the "fool" help to overcome the duality of the mind and body Yamaguchi (1988). Restoring the "fool's" sensibility as a critic of science and civilization serves to balance the relationship between authority, productivity and theory.

There are numerous ways to fragment the world or universe by examining it in a fixed state, ruling over nature, controlling society and using concepts in their narrowest and so-called strictest sense, though there are very few ways to restore the sensibilities of the "fool". Intelligence in the twenty-first century is fundamentally based on expert classification (fragmentation), principles of seriousness (consistency) and a doctrine of strictness (over-emphasis), and any culture that invokes this form of intelligence finds itself imposed with these three criteria.

The intelligence associated with the "fool" as "trickster" should inform us of the futility of subscribing to a single reality. If the desire to be concerned with only a single reality is driven as a result of seeking coherence, then the process of denying a single reality and freely living in and moving between multiple realities to perpetually reveal the hidden features can be considered a type of spiritual technology that develops more dynamic cosmological dimensions. The "trickster" has attracted psychoanalysts like Jung and mythologists like Lévi-Strauss (2013) due to this character's hidden potential to revive and invigorate the universe. We cannot underestimate the importance of the role played by the theory of the "trickster" within Lévi-Strauss's work on myths. Lévi-Strauss famously understood that the "trickster" served as the most effective method at arriving at a mythological conclusion that could resolve the conflict between the many opposing forces at play.

The psychological misfit is the same as the "trickster". Every single one of us seeks to take revenge on those who—underneath the trappings of civilization—indulge in carnality, freedom, gluttony and sexuality, who give themselves up to impulse and mock us. This is the role that the "trickster" assumes. The trickster acts as our champion, excites us, while also serving as a scapegoat (Yamaguchi 1988). It is only through these "mythological others" that we are able to establish a social identity, and this in itself poses a dilemma. In this way, at its root, culture is activated by the elements that try to deny it symbolically and semiotically. This is what grounds and will ground culture.

3.5 Centre and Periphery

In the past, as a result of its influence under functionalism, design was limited to the superficial—to that which could easily be described as the subject of research. It is necessary to adjust our definition of design in terms of its relationship to its own depth. The term "depth" here includes its meaning within psychoanalysis. Rather than strategically limiting design to the superficial, it is necessary to approach design in a way that incorporates into its depth the world captured by all the ability of each individual to make full use of their inhabited space.

The superficial refers to areas that are simple to observe in the field of design research, for these are fields that can be systemized, can be easily articulated through writing and are easy to organize in the form of text. This may enable us to understand superficial systems of communication that are considered indispensable to design. However, there are clearly areas that cannot be overlooked when dealing with how individuals fundamentally interact with their internal and external environment, though these areas be difficult to articulate through language or discuss systematically. However, it is impossible to grasp the meaning of design on a comprehensive level while turning a blind eye to these areas.

The theory of functionalism has dominated mainstream thought for the last 20 years. Functionalism examines the overall functionality of design and examines how the various factors and methodologies that make up the design (on a superficial level) relate to one another. In a way, it is similar to anatomy, in that it observes the body from the outside. While the human body is divided into various parts, they all work together and influence one another, resulting in smooth operation across the entire organism. Functionalism is based on this type of organismic theory. Using this methodology, functional research into design has been able to effectively explain constant factors within design. While this functional explanation is able to clarify the skeletal framework of design, it is not able to visualize the mental images of everyday people.

According to Yamaguchi (2000), people tend to divide culture into one of two fundamental groups: as belonging to their side or as belonging to the other side. People refer to positive things as a part of culture, while they relegate the negative to nature (in other words, the "savage"). For example,

- When listening to various sounds, people classify (random) noise and ordered sound which can give a basis for a scale.

- When looking at lines that are not clearly part of an illustration, people are able to create order through outlines, circles and triangles, which then forms the foundation for communication.

Human consciousness and thought are fundamentally built on the basic process of distinguishing between culture and nature.

Design has a "centre" where systemization and conceptualization are made possible. Viewed from the "centre", it is clear that design has fixed limits in terms of what is possible to systemize. This realm of design can be contrasted with the "non-design" that spreads around its "periphery". Ouspensky (1997) refers to the central, systemized, organized realm as "information", and outlying realms as "entropy". Seen from the "periphery", it is clear that design and "non-design" share a mutually defined boundary—they need one another. In other words, the mechanisms of design function to organize the disorganized, enlighten the unenlightened, purify the sinful and convert entropy into information (Yamaguchi 2000), for example,

- A carnival or other such ritual that transforms "culture" back into "nature"
- Maturation rituals and other initiation rituals that turn a child (an unrefined being, considered neither a god nor an animal) into a "human being"; masks that transform the superficial human (within culture) into something deeper (outside of culture)
- Clothing that transforms an animal (specifically, its pelt) into something human
- Punishments that reduce a human to a sub-human
- Homes that transform an "outside" space into an "inner" space

For designs that reiterate the centre and periphery, the "chaos" of the "periphery" is not necessarily a target for abolition, rather it is indispensable as a model for the "periphery" that is reproduced in the "centre". While design attempts to eradicate the "periphery" present in the centre due to it being a form of "disorder", the periphery as an opposing concept must be reproduced in order for the centre to maintain itself. In design, the "periphery" plays an essential role as a scapegoat for the "centre".

However, the border between the "centre" and the "periphery" is not fixed. The systemized "centre" of design constantly attempts to erode and take in the "periphery". The vitality and polysemy of the "periphery" become the driving force that propels the border with the "centre". In other words, the overarching role of design is to establish the connection point between the "centre" and the "periphery", and subtly shift the position of the border. Areas with a systemized order known as the "centre" include engineering design, system design and strategic design. These concepts have dominated the design field over the last 20 to 30 years due to their high productivity and their compatibility with our information-based society.

While the vitality and polysemy of the "periphery" ideally serve as a driving force to activate the border of the centre, design has become a tool to serve system science, engineering and business. As such, the vitality of genuine design is lost. Design should serve as a challenger that reinvigorates the "centre" through its vitality and ability to provoke. In other words, in order to be perceived as an invigored society in itself, design must be sufficiently provocative in the periphery, and the designer must be able to actively go back and forth through the mechanism of the connection point between the "centre" and the "periphery".

Vitality and polysemy decline if the regularity, averageness and normality of the "centre" continue uninterrupted. The vitality of culture is ensured through the conflict between the "centre" and concepts divorced from the cultural context (such as *infantile play*, the *heterogeneous* and the *latent/unconscious*). Provocativeness is only achieved through being different.

All cultures are fundamentally based around a continual division of the human environment between the "centre" and "periphery", the inside and outside, the preferable and not preferable, and the near and far. In other words, in order to strengthen the identity of people and our culture, we unconsciously create dualities. This becomes clear when observing a child's developmental process Yamaguchi (2000). When developing a conscious awareness of the outside world, infants are able to instinctively classify those who are close to them and those who are not. As a provider of intimate contact, the mother is seen as close and familiar by children, though they are fearful of things with which they have no contact, or that are strange or distant. Even before developing speech, people tend to divide the world between the inner and outer. In the process of our development and education, we find the things in the world that are preferable to be close—or central—to us, and associate these things with our identity. That which is not preferable is pushed far away onto the "periphery". To put it another way, the "centre" and the "periphery" are associated with order and disorder, or the friendly and the hostile. The presence of hostility makes people aware of that which is inner—or "central"—to them on a fundamental level to elucidate its boundary.

We must consider why the "periphery" is excluded and considered unpleasant despite being impossible to think of the "centre" without the "periphery". For example, the political and legal systems (the superficial parts of culture) include a basic understanding of the rules involved, and there is a clear purpose and meaning behind the actions that we take. There are "definitions". The act of "defining" has the effect of keeping one thing while excluding another. That which is ambiguous or undefinable is excluded, whereby a system of order is established. Parts that are excluded due to their indefinability are subject to repeated exclusion (however many times they are debated).

Take the moral and the amoral person, for example. The moral person is easy to define, since that which is "good" is predictable and reliable in any given situation. The amoral person is difficult to define, since their actions are unpredictable and ambiguous. Regardless of the culture, this ambiguity is a target for exclusion.

3.6 Concluding Comments

In an interdisciplinary context, design is ambiguous and difficult to define. As such, it is marginalized. The more one tries to define design, the further it lands from its mark. This is because design (or design culture) is not to be seen to be built on a fixed state of balance; rather, it is conceptualized as an infringement of regulated, organized boundaries. Historically, the Renaissance and Bauhaus periods are obvious examples.

People have an aversion to the unstable, changing or mixed. The loss of form also constitutes a change. Something may briefly take a specific agreed-upon form, but can fall apart regardless of human will and transform into something else in a process of transition. People become unstable when placed in such a transitional state. People are at their most physiologically and mentally unstable during periods of change or transition. The "rite of passage" is a ritualistic system that reinforces the process by which people transition from birth to death. In Japan, this is systemized through the rituals of *Shichigosan* (celebration of children's third, fifth and seventh year of age) and *Yakudoshi* (unlucky ages). Coming of age ceremonies are commonly performed throughout the world. Generally, these ceremonies are held at the most unstable periods of human mental growth before maturity. This period of physical and mental transition marks a shift from order to disorder. Holding these youth-based ceremonies in conditions where people are in instability marks an attempt to neutralize unstable feelings and prevent the loss of identity by giving a form to this transition.

"Mixed" is an empty state that occurs during this transition. People are averse to this unstable state. Expressed in terms of time, dawn and twilight are two states of transition. Twilight provides a sense of freedom from order, while dawn reveals human vitality emerging beyond order, like that of a weed. We dislike weeds because they grow and invade the order of fields. They ignore the rules. Moreover, they are highly fertile and full of vitality.

Seen from the "centre" design is either feared or it is simply used to serve. This is because design provokes instability, transition and mixtures. In human culture, the target of exclusion tends to be seen as something negative. However, it is an intimate and indispensable element for the depth of human psychology. If we see design (the designer) to take the role of the "trickster" in connecting these two parts and arriving at a synthesis, the work of the designer is to transcend time and look into the "periphery", using it as a fulcrum to assemble new models of totality. The process of looking into the future past unstable elements may feel uncomfortable, and this process may become the target of exclusion. However, there is a richness to the polysemy of the "periphery", and by using it as a stepping stone for overcoming boundaries, one discovers the existence of new possibilities.

To date, research into design has eliminated from its focus of research anything that cannot be considered to be the "centre" and that is commonly excluded. These excluded areas challenge that which is ordered and fixed. Without these provocative elements, the ingenuity of design cannot be grasped. The more these excluded aspects are perpetually pushed into the margins of consciousness, space and time, the more they reject the homogeneity that leads to a unified culture. This rejection signifies the dynamic relationship between the "centre" and the "periphery".

Genuine design is entropy that aims to deconstruct order (Hosoe et al. 1991). However, entropy is unable to continue to survive alone. Rather, it fulfils a role as an activator for the mere shell of order that is present within the dynamics of the structure. Design faces the chaos of the "periphery" and confronts its own rebirth as an intermediary between the "centre" and the margins.

References

Colomina B, Wigley M (2016) Are we human? Notes on an archaeology of design. Lars Müller Publishers, Zürich, Switzerland
Comte A (1855) The positive philosophy of Auguste Comte. Calvin Blanchard
Hosoe I, Marinelli A, Sias R (1991) Play office: toward a new culture in the workplace. G.C. Inc. Retrieved from https://ihd.it/portfolio/play-office/
Jung CG (2014) The archetypes and the collective unconscious. Routledge
Levi-Strauss C (1966) The savage mind. University of Chicago Press
Lévi-Strauss C (2013) Myth and meaning. Routledge
Ouspensky PD (1997) A new model of the universe. Courier Corporation
Yamaguchi M (1988) Chi no Shukusai. Kawaideshoboshinsha, Tokyo
Yamaguchi M (1993) Doke No Minzokugaku. Chikuma Shobo, Tokyo
Yamaguchi M (2000) 2000. Iwanami Shoten, Bunka no Ryougi-sei. Tokyo

Chapter 4
Emptiness, Nothingness and the Interval in Between

> *The wonderful part about his paintings was the use of blank space. Paradoxically, the best part was what was not depicted.*
> Haruki Murakami, *Killing Commendatore* (2018)

Abstract We discuss the perception of emptiness from the perspective of Japanese culture, because in the West "emptiness" has different, more limited meanings, with only negative cultural associations such as boredom, meaninglessness and more generally a lack of anything valuable. Why has Japan produced a culture with such a different view of emptiness? The answer can be found in a concept familiar to every Japanese person: "MA". MA is universal and refers to both the interval, which gives shape to the whole, and the whole itself. In the second part of the chapter, we discuss the singularity and universality of MA in relation to design. The MA concept can be seen as the purest essence of distinctly Japanese thought. MA is time and space. The two cannot be considered separately. MA underlies almost everything and is an important component of communication. MA has no substantive meaning. Here we will attempt to reveal the hidden semantics intrinsic to a work of MA.

4.1 Introduction

As Kenya Hara said, "emptiness is richer than fullness". Consider the covers of two of the most influential music albums of the twentieth century by The Beatles: Sgt. Pepper's Lonely Hearts Club Band of 1967 and The White Album (official name, The Beatles) of 1968. The former is a crowded display of riotous colour and elaborate ornamentation. The latter, in stark contrast, is empty, blank whiteness with only the title (which is also the artists' name) embossed in small, white letters. The former promises sugar and spice and psychedelically colourful songs, which is what is on the record inside. The latter promises that almost any style and mood of popular music could be found within, and so it is. Emptiness carries enormous promise, but is also feared: we fill empty time and space with objects and sounds and phone calls and Facebook, because emptiness brings the uncertainty of unresolved possibilities—the very essence of creative potential. Emptiness, then, can be promising or threatening.

© Springer Nature Switzerland AG 2020

K. Hoshi and J. Waterworth, *Primitive Interaction Design*,
Human–Computer Interaction Series,
https://doi.org/10.1007/978-3-030-42954-6_4

As Nagarjuna, the early Buddhist philosopher taught, "Emptiness wrongly grasped is like picking up a poisonous snake by the wrong end".

Most designers, like most other people, are generally limited by the unconscious cultural grip of living in their own particular world, a world of conceptual thought, judgment and belief, or a world of the remembered past and imagined future—in other words, an ideologically generated world. They are absorbing impressions into the internal world of their thoughts and imagination based on their cultural environment. This gives them a sense of self beyond the present moment. But it also produces a separation from the external world and breaks the natural flow of action that is based on constant activity while awake. When functioning smoothly, humans act through largely unconscious motor behaviours; they attend to the here and now without thinking (much), and have a sense of almost complete absorption in what we call contextual emptiness, the external world of the present.

In this chapter, we discuss the perception of emptiness from the perspective of Japanese culture, because in the West "emptiness" has different, more limited meanings, with only negative cultural associations such as boredom, meaninglessness and more generally a lack of anything valuable. Why has Japan produced a culture with such a different view of emptiness? The answer can be found in a concept familiar to every Japanese person: "MA". MA is universal and refers to both the interval, which gives shape to the whole, and the whole itself. In the second part of the chapter, we discuss the singularity and universality of MA in relation to design. The MA concept can be seen as the purest essence of distinctly Japanese thought. MA is time and space. The two cannot be considered separately. MA underlies almost everything and is an important component of communication. MA has no substantive meaning. Here we will attempt to reveal the hidden semantics intrinsic to a work of MA.

In Japanese arts and architecture, MA epitomizes the dynamic balance between object and space, action and inaction, sound and silence, and movement and rest. We explore why Japanese classic artists and architects historically have used MA as the consummate concept, while western arts have had little interest in MA, and why there is no general understanding of MA in western culture. We explore the principles and process of creation in MA. MA can be described as a creative space, which opens and closes, swells and contracts as though it were endowed with unlimited functional flexibility.

4.2 Emptiness, Nothingness and the Interval in Between

This section concerns emptiness, nothingness and the interval in between, which may all be understood as having the same meaning, and how "ma" (interval in between), have evolved in the consciousness of daily life from historical and cultural backgrounds.

It is speculated that Buddhism was introduced to China around the 1st Century BC, and it is said that the translation of Buddhist scriptures began in earnest in the second half of the 2nd Century (Kimura 2004). At that time, the central issue in the

Buddhist world was how to interpret the philosophy of "nothingness" of Taoism, which had attracted the hearts of people instead of Confucianism, using Buddhist concepts (Kimura 2004). In the Chinese ideological world at that time, the Prajnaparamita Sutras were spreading wide ripples, and they tried to understand the idea of "emptiness" preached by the Prajnaparamita Sutra with reference to Taoism's idea of "nothingness". After that, Buddhism was introduced to Japan, and it is said that the idea of "emptiness" was established as "impermanence" or "deficiency".

In Buddhism that developed in Japan, concepts like "impermanence" and "deficiency" were first established. The deficiency philosophy represented by Japanese classical literature (Tsurezuregusa) created beauty that included suggestiveness, aftertastes and blank space as artistic consciousness. In the case of physical art, it also created "ma" as spaces between music and performance as well as rhythm and pause in martial arts. These "ma" have evolved apart from their matrix such as impermanence, and they were developed along with the "ma" of the consciousness in daily life (Kenmochi 1992).

What we usually consider "exists" is in relation to other things, and there is nothing that autonomously exists on its own. Therefore, there is nothing in the real world that we can say "exists" with absolute certainty. Because "exists" itself is established in a relationship with "does not exist", saying "exists" or "does not exist" itself is something that does not exist absolutely (Yokoyama 2002).

4.3 Deficiency and Impermanence

Deficiency and impermanence are not negative views. Unlike views like the Western absolute truth that creates a perfect world or the absolute rule of science by rationalism, "impermanence" is a worldview that observes that things in existence are constantly changing, and it is to see that things those have a shape will eventually disappear. This was called "emptiness" in Mahayana Buddhism (Yokoyama 2002).

If the absolute rule by rationalism is a fulfilment principle that fills "ma", then recognizing "ma", perceiving the meaning of silence that cannot be expressed in words and denying rationalistic sense of fulfilment can be called deficiency. It can also be called an aesthetic state of mind that does not require eternity from fulfilment. It is difficult to spend time on a detailed discussion of how the idea of "emptiness" was inherited from early Buddhism to Mahayana Buddhism, how it was developed and accepted in Mahayana Buddhism, and how the Buddhist world of East Asia, especially China, has perceived "emptiness" and transformed it into its own independent thought. Since this is not directly in line with the subject of this book, further discussion will be reserved for another time.

4.3.1 Nietzsche's Nihilism

Nietzsche's nihilism (Nietzsche and Common 1950) is famous as a representative concept of "nothingness" in Western thought. Nihilism is a worldview that refers to a meaningless state that has lost ideals and values. For Nietzsche, "nothingness" was absence, and nihilism was thorough absence. It is the emptiness of where "God" has collapsed, who was the ultimate support of the meaning of living as the highest ground for bringing everything into existence, and it is nihilism and meaninglessness of "eternal meaninglessness". It can be said that it is distinct from the concept of "nothingness" in the East, which has been developed as artistic consciousness and daily life consciousness.

4.3.2 The Ordinariness, Logic and Structure of "Ma"

"Ma" is a word that is being used without thinking deeply or having doubts about its meaning. It is a word or concept that refers to one of the characteristics of Japanese people and Japanese culture and is also perceivable. "Ma" is commonly found in everyday life, martial arts, or sports and art.

The Japanese perceive the subtle pathos of "ma" as a form of consciousness in everyday life, sports, art and even religion as the foundation, especially Zen. It is not just physical and physiological processes such as rest, silence or gaps. It is an experience that cannot be expressed in words or shapes, and it can be said to be a perception that transcends consciousness. At least in Western culture, there is no clear equivalent to it.

Natural science, which evolved from Greek philosophy, assumes that all phenomena in the world consist of the connection of things. It is said that the act of connecting zero intervals between entities forms the scientific world. The basic structure of "ma" can be represented as shown in Fig. 4.1 (Shiozawa 1986). The circles in the figure represent entities. The reason for using a circle to represent an entity is that the ultimate shape of a thing is considered to be a spherical particle.

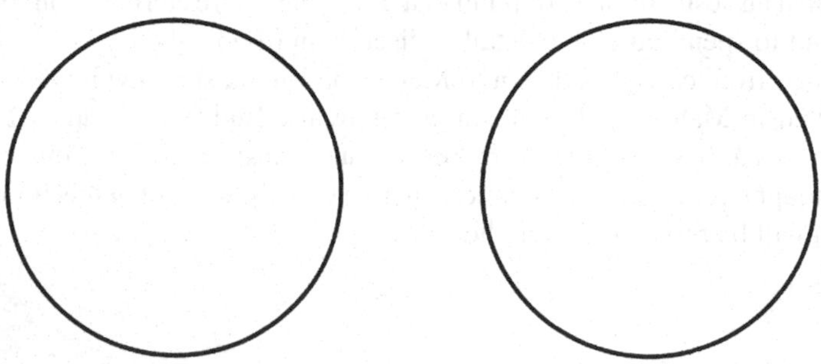

Fig. 4.1 The structure of "ma"

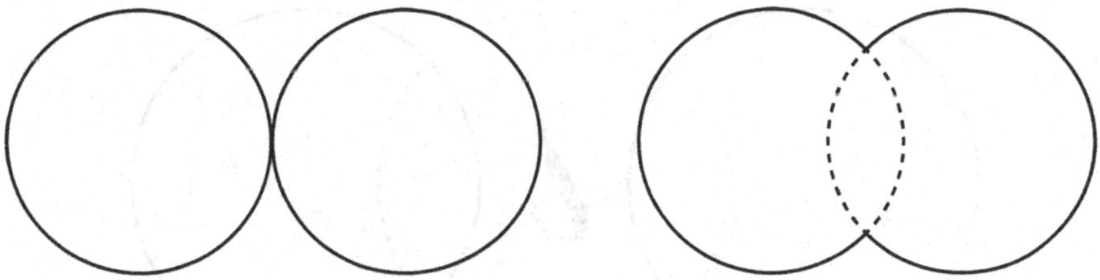

Fig. 4.2 Conditions for connection in natural science

The positional relationship where the two circles are separated from each other represents a state where they are not in physical contact. As shown in Fig. 4.1, in order for "ma" to be established, a minimum of two things should exist and they should be separated from each other.

The logic of "ma" takes the position that there is some connection between the two circles in Fig. 4.1. In contrast, the position of materialism of natural science, which is that there is no connection between the separated circles, is the complete opposite of the logic of "ma". In the materialism of natural science, the following two conditions must be met for a connection to be established.

- The circles must have shared points, lines or areas.
- The above must be on or within both circles.

This relationship can be expressed as in Fig. 4.2.

But the logic of "ma" cannot be explained in materialism of natural science. It is necessary to recognize the existence of a third party other than the two circles and discuss this existence as a concept that goes beyond materialism of natural science. It then becomes possible to establish a relationship between two circles and a third party.

In the logic of "ma", the existence of this third party was temporarily set to "i". "i" means an imaginary number in mathematics, but "i" can also mean *image*, *information* and *interest*, as well as *invisible*, a concept beyond natural science materialism. "i" can be regarded as "emptiness" with an infinite extent.

Since the structure in which the invisible emptiness of "i" is between two entities and connects the two entities is visually represented only as the entities, and what intervenes cannot be captured, it is visualized by only two entities, as shown in Fig. 4.3. It indicates that there is an invisible "i" between entities. Depending on the consciousness of the viewer, it will have unlimited openness.

Take the form of communication of shaking hands and bowing. A handshake is a greeting given to a person by grasping other's hand. At that time, the communication between the two is in the form of connection expressed in Fig. 4.2. Bowing, on the other hand, is a greeting where both parties do not touch each other and is a form of connection that places a spatial "i" between them, as shown in Fig. 4.3. The handshake became popular in Western culture and bowing developed in Japan, where the logic of "ma" is pervasive in everyday life. The world of materialism of

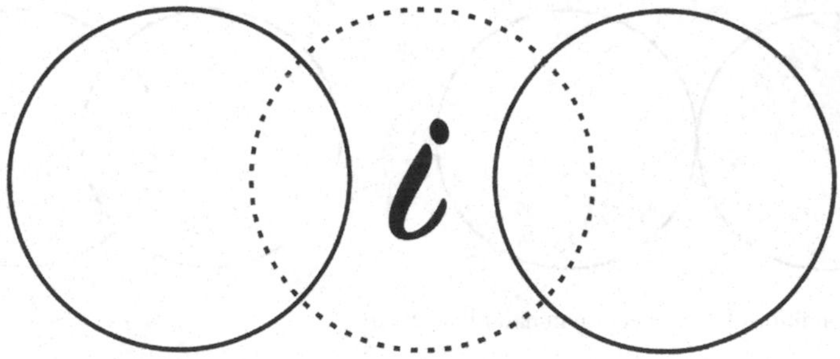

Fig. 4.3 An invisible connection between two entities

natural science demands or seeks certainty, stability and rules. Spatiotemporal gaps are said to be a cause of anxiety, uncertainty and instability. In the world of the logic of "ma", it is normal for there to be spatiotemporal gaps, and "ma" and "emptiness" are provided to ensure freedom of behaviour and consciousness.

4.4 "i" for Art

"i" is an empty entity, but it is not the same as nothingness. Nothingness means there is nothing at all. "i" does not mean that there is nothing at all, but instead, "nothing" does "exist". In nothingness anything is "non-existent", whereas "i" means that there is the "existence" of the entity of "nothing". "0" does not mean there is nothing. There is a "nothing" that exists; that is why it is "0". "i" is an existence called "nothing".

Looking at Japanese architecture, Taut (1934) was deeply impressed and surprised that "emptiness" is valued and plays an important role in architecture. In particular, his attention was drawn by the fact that there was usually nothing placed in a Japanese tearoom, and it was kept "empty". In Western culture, rooms are decorated with ornaments such as curtains, furniture, figurines, paintings and vases. A tearoom, on the other hand, is empty. From that, he saw the spirit of traditional Japanese beauty, different from the West.

Hall (1966) compared the Western way of reasoning with "ma", and explains as follows: When Westerners think and talk about space, they keep in mind the distance between things. In the West, we are taught to perceive and react to the arrangement of things and to consider space to be "empty". The meaning of this is apparent when compared to the Japanese. Japanese are trained to perceive the shape and arrangement of space and give meaning to space. This is represented by the word "ma". This space called "ma" is the fundamental architectural break in all spatial experiences of the Japanese people. In Western Europe, people perceive objects but not the space in between them. In Japan, space is perceived, named and respected as "ma", in essence, intervening space.

The culture of perceiving "ma" is built on a tension that minimizes entities to the utmost. Using only one brush and one colour of ink to draw a scene that would have used various brush touches and as much colour as possible if it was an oil painting, or a sentiment that can extend across hundreds of manuscript papers if written but has been reduced to just 17 or 31 characters as a Haiku or Tanka. The more something is minimized, the heavier the importance of each line and each character becomes, and the spaces between the lines and the characters also become more important. In music, a selected "ma" is placed between the sounds as an interval of silence with tension. In the tea ceremony, value is placed on the clarity of the place where evil is filtered away.

The logic of "ma" forces strict choices. The more serious the choice, the higher the tension in the spirit. The real "i" comes from a process of strict choice for a limited entity. The choices here form the basis of the individual's independent activities and differ from the objective approach. This is respect for independence, and it is not as if AI is automatically processing it from big data. They are self-empirical, embodied and introspective choices.

The characteristic of the concept of "ma" in the structure of Japanese consciousness is that it is not a blank state or a situation where something that should be there is missing, but it is rather a positive creation. Because "ma" is a creation, it lives in daily life and in the essence of art. For example, Japanese literature such as Waka (和歌) and Haikai (俳諧) has been able to incorporate the excellent art of "ma" because the consciousness of "ma" has been nurtured as the foundation of the Japanese way of thinking itself. As a result, Japanese performing arts were also able to form customs like the Noh (能) dance and tea ceremony (茶道) (Shiozawa 1986).

4.4.1 *The Root of Creativity*

It is the Japanese perspective that there is "ma" in nature. The "wind" is considered as the breaths of nature, and the "ma" between those breaths is called "Kazama ("ma" of wind)". In Japan, nature is often expressed by the word "wind (風)", in words such as "landscape (風景)", "topography (風土)" and "scenic beauty (風光)" (Kenmochi 1992). It can be inferred that the characteristics of Japan's climate depend on the wind direction in each season, so the Japanese became particularly sensitive to the wind. Because the wind blows through empty space, it matches the Japanese sense of "ma".

4.4.2 *Seasonal Feeling*

Historically in Europe, the focus has been on day and night. The March equinox and the September equinox, when the length of day and night are equal, are, respectively, called the beginning of spring and the beginning of autumn. The winter solstice and summer solstice, when difference of length of day and night becomes maximum, are, respectively, called the beginning of winter and the beginning of summer. The four seasons in Europe and the sense of the seasons are categories defined by quantitative natural science, whereas the Japanese perceive the transition of the four seasons "qualitatively" and perceive "ma" between the seasons.

4.4.3 *Topography*

The topography of Japan, an island country with many mountains, is densely populated in narrow plains, with cultivated land being managed intensively and with horticultural delicacy. There are almost no monotonous elements in Japan's climate and topography, and there are always many changes. The vibrancy of Japan's nature is something that foreigners who have come to Japan all mention. Japanese have had to live with nature and accept natural disasters such as typhoons, earthquakes, heavy rains, heatwaves and heavy snow. Japan's nature is constantly moving. The Japanese perceive nature as though it smiles and talks to us like human beings. The Japanese embodied over a long period of time the diversity and the quickness of changes in nature.

There are four seasons in Europe, but severe changes and sudden natural disasters that overwhelm people are rare. The conditions of being an island nation of the same ethnicity and language and being blessed with nature that is varied and rich in vitality, in which we must survive through farming and fishing, engrained the particular ability of communication into the Japanese. Dialogue among people and dialogue between people and nature is of the same dimension. Nature speaks to people, and people speak to nature. People can talk to other people through and entrusting nature. From Japan's topography, geographical conditions, sharing of the same language and natural conditions, it can be inferred that the language of silence, the perception of the meaning of emptiness and the language of speaking without words were inevitably established. Formation of the perception and structure of "ma" also accompanies these backgrounds.

4.5 Decorative Space and Lyrical Space

Historically, European spatial culture has created decorative spaces, and Japanese culture has created lyrical spaces. In the consciousness of the Europeans, space should be decorated with something. Stained glass is inserted into a dome to let in the light. A hall is decorated with a chandelier to fill the space itself with the effects of the light. They do not allow for empty space. If there is a place to reminisce, they will place various portraits, paintings and memorabilia.

A Japanese tearoom is completely empty, except for things placed for a little while to fulfil the satisfaction of aesthetic feelings. Extraordinary items are brought in temporarily, and everything else is selected so as to blend to enhance the beauty of the centrepiece. People cannot listen to various kinds of music at the same time. A true understanding of a beautiful object can only be achieved by focusing one's attention on a central point. We can see that the decoration method of the tearoom culture is different from the decoration method of Western culture, where an interior can often start becoming a museum. For people who are used to the tearoom culture with its simplicity of decor and frequent changes in the elements of decor, a Western interior that is permanently filled with numerous displays of paintings, sculptures and antiques can give a feeling of merely showing off wealth.

"People who are used to the tearoom culture with…frequent changes in the elements of decor" replace flower arrangements and hanging scrolls as appropriate for the season. Harmony with the seasons is achieved by making use of "ma". This is what a *lyrical space* is about, and it is a major difference between the decorative spaces.

4.5.1 Tearoom, Tea Garden and "Ma"

Intellectuals of Japanese culture and art have pointed out how well the structure of a tearoom shows the essence of Japanese culture, especially in the context of a tea garden. In particular, they emphasize the similarity between the structure of a "tea garden and tearoom" and Waka, in that one gazes at the tea garden outside the tearoom and enters the tearoom through the tea garden. The tea garden summarizes the Japanese landscape. However, if one steps inside the tearoom, the window is a shoji screen that shrouds the view of the scenery outside. In the quiet tearoom, one can hear that the sound of hot water boiling resembles the sound of the wind blowing through pine trees. This is the transition from the visual world (tea garden) to the auditory world (tearoom).

This is similar to the transition from the visual world of the 5/7/5 syllable format of the upper verse in a Waka to the auditory world of the 7/7 syllable format of the lower verse, or to the inner world. Waka is also an art of "ma" In the subtle "ma" between the upper and lower verses, there is a sense of harmony and diversion, which gives a clue as to the understanding of the art of "ma".

4.5.2 Dance

Although almost everyone in Japan feels, creates and plays the aesthetics of "ma" and it is a very familiar thing, it is not always noticeable. Such "ma" has various forms of expression depending on the genre style. What are the common basic conditions of "ma?" "Ma" is a sense of distance when something is being cut temporally and spatially. It varies in size but has this basic condition in common.

The sense of the beauty of "ma" created by the Japanese is something unique because we discovered the sense of beauty created by a disconnection in this spatiotemporal "ma" not just the sense of beauty in interlocking and continuous dynamism. The most important condition of "ma" is this disconnection. In other words, it can be said that "ma" is a sense of beauty created by a sense of distance due to a spatiotemporal cut.

The sense and concept of "ma" are extremely Japanese. It is often emphasized that the existence of a "ma" is a characteristic of Japanese performing arts and culture in general (Taut 1934 and Hall 1966).

In dance, "ma" refers to a stationary state, and the transition of a movement is also included in "ma". In modern dance and ballet, we value the flow of one movement and "ma" when moving from one movement to another. In other words, in Western dance, the emphasis is on how to move. This is generally called "rhythm" (Minami 1983).

Japanese Noh rhythms have complex and detailed rules, but whether singing or dancing, performing Noh embodies the rhythm of putting oneself in an infinite time period that transcends self-consciousness (subconsciousness). Zeami (2012) wrote in "Kakyo", "Forget the voice and know the song, forget the song and know the tone, forget the tone and know the rhythm". The experience of a dancer placing himself or herself in an infinite time period in a subconscious state is where the rhythm of dance reaches. It can be said that a Japanese dancer experiences dance in "quietness", while a Western dancer experiences it in "movement". In traditional Japanese art, masters pursued this existence of "nothing". Zeami called it "senuhima" ("interval of no-action") (Zeami 2012).

The consciousness of the deepest tensions in the mind attentively connects the arts and crafts. The gap where one stops dancing, the gap where one stops singing a song, and the moments of pause in all other arts such as dialogue and gestures, which enhance the depth of attentiveness with plenitude of consciousness maintaining tension, are called "senuhima". "Senuhima" is nothing, but instead, it is "a deep sense of fulfilment that maintains tension".

There is also an expression called "shijima" ("silence"). The sounds produced by hitting or plucking disappear one by one and leave a lingering sound. The ears of Japanese musicians have found musical significance in "shijima", which is found after the disappearance of the lingering sound. Encountering endless silence following the lingering sound, they listened to the tension in that "shijima" and caught it in the silence between the sounds (Minami 1983).

4.6 Mind and Communication

In "Beyond Culture", Hall (1989) classifies the types of language communication around the world into high-context and low-context cultures. A low-context culture trusts the power of words, with the conviction that the correct use of words will transmit what is in one's mind. There is absolute trust that "if I use words rationally,

Table 4.1 High and low-context cultures

High-context culture	**Low-context culture**
• Indirect and ambiguous • Important information is not (or may not be) expressed with words • Conversation based on common recognition • Understanding of non-verbal "ma" • Emotional decision-making • Silent "ma" is not a break but part of the context	• Clear and detailed • All information is expressed and presented with words • Verbal-based conversation • Non-verbal components are not perceived or included in the conversation • Logical decision-making • Silence is a break and is unpleasant
Example high-context cultures Japan Asian countries Arab world Southern Europe	**Example low-context cultures** Switzerland Germany Scandinavia North America

the other party can communicate rationally as well". However, for the Japanese, there is an implicit consciousness that we cannot communicate our minds by words alone. The unspoken "implication", which is not expressed by words, is more highly valued subconsciously, and the perception and structure of "ma" are incorporated. High-context cultures include Japan, Asia and Arabic countries, and Japanese is referred to as the most extreme language. Low-context cultures include Switzerland, Germany, Scandinavia and the United States, with German being the most extreme language (Table 4.1).

Science has so far explored only the physical "entity". From now on, the search for "ma" must be included as well. "ma" is not a position to negate or confront science but rather aims to inherit scientific exploration and encourage new creations. The current limitations of science to entities and their associations should be removed, and a more liberal universality should be sought. In the process of pursuing the objective facts of entities and their associations, science has called for abandoning the concepts of self and ordinariness and becoming a third party in order to know the essence of an entity or association. The quest for "ma" aims to revive the concepts of self and ordinariness and take a subjective approach. Taking advantage of self and ordinariness must be much more universal.

4.7 "Ma" in Design

Design is thought to inspire and impress people's consciousness, but when things or systems are used in a natural flow or in such an environment or situation, people become unaware of those things and do not consider themselves as "users" who use them. Certain things disappear from perception and people subconsciously try to harmonize with things and their environment. When walking on a crowded pedestrian crosswalk, people are unaware of the shoes or socks they are wearing and are not consciously thinking about the ground while walking. On the noisy crosswalk, pedestrians walk across without colliding with each other. "Ma" is subconsciously perceived and each route is created there. "Ma" blends into subconscious acts. People are constantly and subconsciously seeking opportunities to maintain balance with things, systems, the environment and nature. It is also creative. People are creative by nature. To design is to provide "ma" and forego awareness of things that exist in the flow. **The "ma" in design** is what is created in a subconscious interaction, which exists during the process of dynamic interaction between people and their environment, where we extract information from our accumulated physical experience, classify it and bring it back into our body.

Gibson (2014) attempted to demonstrate the act of subconsciously finding value in the environment from the perspective of ecological epistemology. He claimed that people subconsciously integrate with their environment through a series of actions. Lakoff and Johnson (2008) described such subconscious thinking and behaviour from the perspective of cognitive linguistics. He argued and attempted to demonstrate that the mind is originally embodied and thought is mostly subconscious.

Each assertion denies actions given by the knowledge accumulated in an individual's brain at the subconscious level. People are not like robots that cannot act unless all knowledge is prepared in the brain beforehand, and subconscious actions are the process of dynamic interaction between people and their environment.

We tend to think that we always act consciously, but most ordinary everyday activities are subconscious without intervention from our ego. In fact, there are always moments that exist in our ordinary everyday lives where we all behave in the same way subconsciously regardless of our ethnicity or culture.

There is room for debate on topics such as what kinds of phenomena are subconscious and where the boundary is between consciousness and subconsciousness. The next chapter examines the differences between the interpretation of consciousness and subconsciousness in Eastern and Western thought and proposes a universal design approach and its methodology focusing on the collective subconscious actions of human beings.

4.8 Concluding Comments

The meaning of emptiness depends on the context, which refers to the conditions in which a situation or communication exists that make its meaning understandable. Perceptual meaning can be defined by how much the empty space is filled up with contextual cues. For example, such contextual cues as the surroundings, circumstances, environment, background or settings, or more specifically, weight, texture, smell, airflow, sound, light and shadow, may all contribute to a context that facilitates creativity through sensory experiences. By contrast, if a person is in a situation of fully conscious thought and explicit information—for example, absorbed in understanding a complex legal document—there is no space to be filled up with contextual cues (from the five sense faculties), and the person is mentally absent from their current physical situation. The feeling of presence is in the timeless now, through sensory perceptions of objects and other features of the present environment (see also Waterworth and Hoshi 2016).

Part of the unacknowledged design skill in creating successful artefacts and systems stems, ironically, from the fact that in the perception of empty space designers employ not only vision but also their other senses. Olfaction, shifts in temperature, humidity, light, shade and colour work together, so as to enhance the person's whole body as a sensing organ. It is as if their sensory perceptions have developed certain mental capacities of observation. We have explored this notion of emptiness and observation, from the perspective of Buddhist philosophy, and in later chapters discuss just how "emptiness" and other factors affect the experience of presence in the design computer-mediated realities.

References

Gibson JJ (2014) The ecological approach to visual perception: classic edition. Psychology Press
Hall ET (1966) The hidden dimension, vol 609. Doubleday, Garden City, NY
Hall ET (1989) Beyond culture. Anchor
Kenmochi T (1992) Ma no Nihon Bunka. Chobunnsha, Tokyo
Kimura K (2004) Nihon no Tetsugaku, vol 5. Showado
Kunihiko S (1986) Ma no Tetsugaku. Liber Press, Tokyo
Lakoff G, Johnson M (2008) Metaphors we live by. University of Chicago Press
Minami H (1983) Ma no Kenkyu. Kodansha, Tokyo
Nietzsche FW, Common T (1950) Thus Spake Zarathustra. Modern Library, New York
Shiozawa K (1986) Ma no Tetsugaku. Liber Press.
Taut B (1934) Nippon. Meiji-Shobo
Waterworth J, Hoshi K (2016) Human-experiential design of presence in everyday blended reality: living in the here and now. Springer, Switzerland
Yokoyama K (2002) Yasashii yuishiki. NHK SHUPPAN
Zeami (2012) Fushikaden, Kakyo. Tachibana Tokyo

Chapter 5
Unconscious Interaction and Design

> The moment of truth, the sudden emergence of a new insight, is an act of intuition. Such intuitions give the appearance of miraculous flashes, or short-circuits of reasoning. In fact they may be likened to an immersed chain, or which only the beginning and end are visible above the surface of consciousness. The diver vanishes at one end of the chain and comes up at the other end, guided by invisible links.
> Arthur Koestler, *The Act of Creation* (1964).

Abstract This chapter deals with the unconscious, both in interaction and in design. Although the ideal of seamless interaction is that people do not need to think how to use digital technology, design researchers and design practitioners have tended to focus on explicitly revealing problems and solving them. These are problems that they can physically see and linguistically discuss. Although this may involve questions of how to design for mostly unconscious interaction, it does not generally take into account that there are different levels of the world in our everyday life: overt and covert, implicit and explicit, things you can and do talk about, and things you cannot and do not talk about. It is not just that people interact unconsciously and designers seek to achieve this as an aim, it is that there is such a thing as the unconscious, the submerged and unobserved fundament of our psychic existence. Beneath the clearly perceived, highly explicit surface phenomena, there lies a whole other world or even worlds. This applies equally to people interacting and designers (who are people too) designing. Once we understand this, it changes our view of human nature and how to design for and with it.

5.1 Introduction

While Western philosophical thought is descriptive and assembles intricate functional elements to compose nature, in the East, everything is considered as part of nature as a whole, including human beings. Both thoughts complement each other. Since Aristotle, Western philosophy has had a tradition to divide everything precisely by

© Springer Nature Switzerland AG 2020

K. Hoshi and J. Waterworth, *Primitive Interaction Design*,
Human–Computer Interaction Series,
https://doi.org/10.1007/978-3-030-42954-6_5

laws of category, causality and ethics to try to integrate knowledge, whereas in Eastern philosophy, the idea is to stop thinking separately and accept something that cannot be divided—that is, "chaos" and "Alaya-consciousness".

In the East, every living creature, including people, is considered as a part of the whole. People, AI-avatars, Tamagotchi, robots, pets and insects have equal value in the view of the world of innumerableness. In the West, on the other hand, the world is composed of vertical layers according to the degree of intelligence compared with people, with the absolute being at the top, followed then by people. In Eastern thought, especially Buddhism, we explore humanity through our own experiences. Rather than seeking an absolute answer, we explore our mind's responses and their meanings through our personal experiences.

5.1.1 *Everything is Already There*

In Western philosophy, people confront and try to overcome nature. As a result, they think nature is something that can be controlled. On the contrary in Eastern philosophy, it is felt that everything has been there from the beginning. A chaos is already there; everything is equal and everything is born there. What is unique to the East is that there is something that cannot be reached by building up vertical layers, but can exist only when it is regarded as a whole from the beginning. In other words, the West thinks that a design or a designed object is something created by people, whereas the East feels that a design is already there waiting for people to dig it out. It is dug out in the unconsciousness shared by the whole, not consciously.

In the Eastern view of the world, the world is contained within a certain thing which has been there from the beginning, and everything is in there. This is a major principle in Eastern philosophy.

According to Jung (2014), the purpose of dreams is to bring about a reversal in the relationship between self-consciousness and unconsciousness, and to show the unconsciousness as the origin of the personality which is experiencing the reality. The reversal implies that our unconscious existence is the real one, and our conscious world a kind of illusion, an apparent reality constructed for a specific purpose, like a dream which seems a reality as long as we are in it. In short, people in the world are constructing a subjective world that is necessary for their survival. The real world and the world in a dream are very much alike. People are seeing an illusion. It is not an absurd illusion, but rather, an orderly one co-created by self and the environment that surrounds the self. In other words, we act in a real world through the illusion.

One of Jung's great contributions is that he popularized the concept of the collective unconscious common to all ethnic groups and human beings, which cannot be explained by anything in the individual unconscious. He argued that the unconscious has, in addition to our personal subconscious level, which is an accumulation of one's memories and experiences since his/her birth, an ideological level, namely, the collective unconscious that is a collection of knowledge shared by human beings since the day they came to existence. Using an iceberg as a model for human consciousness, he explained that the subconscious under water makes up most of human consciousness and influences individual behaviour by interacting with the mere tip of the iceberg, namely, consciousness. Whether acts of unconsciousness are caused by the collective unconscious has not been scientifically explained. The collective unconscious is a domain shared by all human beings regardless of their nationalities or races. It manifests itself in the ancient myths and legends, art, and personal dreams as well (Lévi-Strauss 2013). It is an aggregated consciousness and a realm of consciousness surpassing space and time. The Buddhist equivalent is Alaya-consciousness.

5.1.2 *Jungian Collective Unconsciousness*

Freud defined the human mind as a whole organ, with a certain size. The mind is divided into a surface level and bottom levels. The unconscious is defined as the deep psyche in the deepest level of the mind. The unconscious, the deep psyche, does not come up to the realm of the conscious. Freud based the existence of the unconscious on a variety of observations such as lapses of memory or slips of the tongue of normal people, or the actions of patients with psychosomatic illnesses. It can be said of the mind that: "I am that I am".

Jung developed Freud's concept further and proposed a realm of unconsciousness that cannot be explained by Freud's theory. He named it the "collective" or "universal" unconscious. He proposed the existence of a collective unconscious that lies in a deeper place than the personal consciousness and is shared by all humanity. See Fig. 5.1.

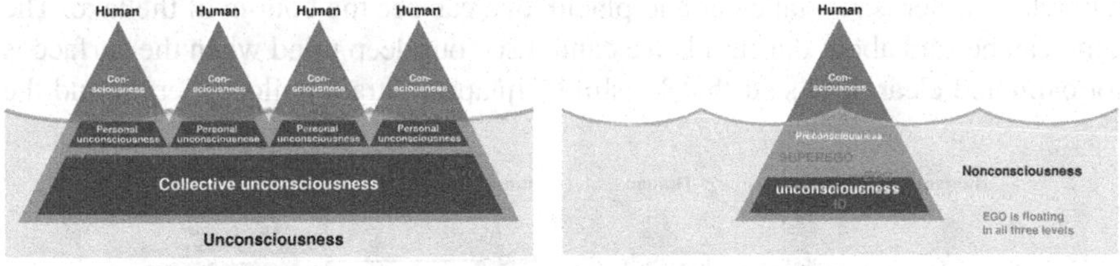

Fig. 5.1 Freudian and Jungian perspectives on the unconscious

5.2 Concepts of the Conscious and the Unconscious

According to the Yuishiki/Vijñapti-mātratā school of Buddhism, on top of the deep mind, there is a surface mind that reflects the deep mind. When the consciousness of the deep mind is clouded, we cannot see things clearly and every affliction may be caused by this cloudiness (see Fig. 5.2). Yuishiki/Vijñapti-mātratā advocates certain practices to clean out the clouded mind. According to de Saussure (2011), the language given by society divides up the world into arbitrary concepts. In Yuishiki/Vijñapti-mātratā, however, it is said that the origin of cognition lies in the deep mind.

According to Yokoyama (2002), the mind is composed of eight consciousnesses from eye-consciousness to Alaya-consciousness. They have no shape or size. Thus, there is no surface layer or deep layer in our mind. Strictly speaking, we cannot call Alaya-consciousness a deep mind. Separating the groups of eyes, ears, nose, tongue, body and mental consciousnesses from Alaya-consciousness, we should call the former the "manifested mind" and the latter the "hidden mind". However, we borrow Freud's term of "deep psyche" and categorize Alaya-consciousness as a deep psyche. Everything manifests as a transformation from the Alaya-consciousness as a deep mind. We can say that all is contained in Alaya-consciousness.

Mind must have cognition objects. Without them, there can never be a subject that cognizes, i.e. consciousness. This echoes the phenomenological view from Husserl (2012, 2013) that consciousness is always consciousness of something (Scott 1972). Consciousness is "something that seems possible, but impossible. Something that seems impossible, but is possible".

5.2.1 *The Function of Consciousness*

When lake water is crystal clear and placid, one can see the bottom of the lake. The same can be said about our mind. We cannot see our deep mind when the surface is not calm and clear. It is said that Yuishiki/Vijñapti-mātratā philosophers found the

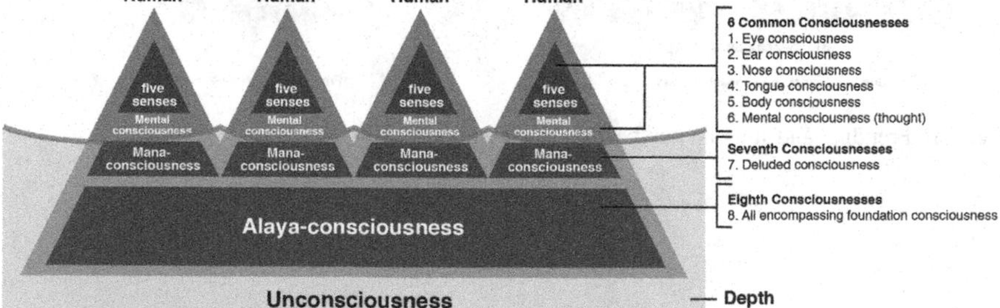

Fig. 5.2 Yuishiki/Vijñapti-mātratā view of the conscious and the unconscious

two layers of the deep mind, namely, Mana-consciousness and Alaya-consciousness by calming down the mind in turmoil through Yoga (a traditional religious practice).

The Yuishiki/Vijñapti-mātratās school added these two consciousnesses to the conventional six (eye, ear, nose, tongue, body and mental) to conjecture the structure of mind as being composed of eight consciousnesses. This is called the "theory of eight consciousnesses" (see Fig. 5.2).

The eight consciousnesses can be categorized into the following four groups:

- Sense consciousnesses:
  - The eye, ear, nose, tongue and body consciousnesses.
  - These consciousnesses grasp objects without language. Each of them has objects unique to them.
- Mental consciousness: Thought
  - Working with the above five consciousnesses, it makes the senses clear. Following the above five, it grasps the objects with language.
- Ego-consciousness: Mana-consciousness
  - Its object is always Alaya-consciousness and it creates "ego" attachment, which can pollute the surface mind.
- Foundation consciousness: Alaya-consciousness
  - It produces the levels from eye-consciousness to Mana-consciousness. It is generated in our body and maintains it physiologically. It creates nature and keeps cognizing it. It has the seeds to create everything.

5.2.2 Existence of the Mind

The "Shiki" in "Yuishiki/Vijñapti-mātratā" means "consciousness", and thus Yuishiki/Vijñapti-mātratā is the same as "mind only". It takes a spiritualist's point of view of "only the mind exists". We have to be careful in that spiritualism here is fundamentally different from that of Western culture. In his subjective idealism, Berkeley argued (1999) that "All that exist are God, the human mind and perception. Other than these, there is nothing of substance. The world consists of the minds of people and perceptions in their minds. Behind the phenomenal world there exists the God that gives us minds". He takes the relative view of presence or absence, wherein "There exists only the mind, and no physical materials exist". The argument that "There exists only the mind" is to prove the existence of God.

For example (from Koichi Yokoyama 1979), supposing there is a chair in front of us, when the eye-consciousness functions, it is engaged to see the chair, simply because there is the chair. If there is no chair, the eye-consciousness to see the chair will be absent. The "eye-consciousness (cognition subject) is present when there is a chair (cognition object), and the eye-consciousness is absent if there is no chair". In other words, the expression "something that seems possible, but impossible. Something that seems impossible, but possible" is correct. Yuishiki/Vijñapti-mātratā philosophers called this "to posit the existence". If we hear "there is only consciousness", we tend to think there should be "something" that corresponds to the consciousness. However, the "consciousness" of Yuishiki/Vijñapti-mātratā consciousness is a posited existence. It does not necessarily exist as a tangible substance. Describing it by noun makes us think there is such a thing; however, if we introspect quietly, we realize that there exists no "consciousness", but merely an act of being aware (verb). It is easier to understand the phenomenon if we use verbs instead of nouns. The fact that "we are looking at a chair" can be realistically described by the simple verb "to look at", rather than using "visual consciousness to see a chair". It may be more realistic to say that only the things that can be described by verbs can exist.

Yuishiki/Vijñapti-mātratā, and Buddhism in broad sense, think that each "consciousness" must have cognition objects of its own. Plato distinguished body from soul by saying that "The human body is the prison of the soul". Descartes divided entities into mind and material. The soul and mind, they argued, are used as the objects of religion. The idea of "something that seems possible, but impossible. Something that seems impossible, but possible" of "shiki-consciousness" is probably more realistic.

5.3 Design and the Structure of Consciousness

Conventionally, design considers Umwelt and human beings separately. People have been designing artefacts in accordance with Descartes' mechanical philosophy in which they first acquire knowledge from the separate Umwelt by using perception sensors and then generate motion via decision-making. The "human" here can be replaced with "intelligence". This world consists of Umwelt and bodies with intelligence, and there is a boundary in between them. In other words, between the body and Umwelt, there is skin, ears, eyes, nose, tongue and senses, and these constitute the boundary to contain intelligence within the body. The body exists in the interface between intelligence and Umwelt, and it can be said that artificial intelligence in general tries to understand the world and intelligence with Descartes' mechanistic philosophy.

Figure 5.3 illustrates the structure of human mind using the iceberg model of the conscious and unconscious. So far, conventional designs have dealt with the realm of human consciousness, which can be objectified fairly easily. It is the design of artefacts applying inferences or calculative thinking. Although the unconscious in the deep mind was not covered as the field for designing, during the last 10 or 20 years, several discussions have been made on artefact design incorporating ecological, physical, phenomenological and cognitive functions.

In principle, a profound exploration into the relation of human cognition, body and environment will accelerate technological advancement, making artefacts that surpass inferences or calculative thinking possible. But we cannot see the world without having illusions. Conscious alone is not enough to grasp the world. This is

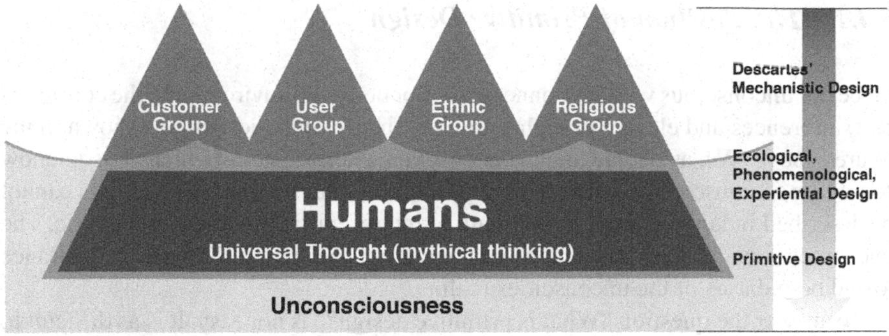

Fig. 5.3 Consciousness/unconsciousness in relation to design and groups

because the conscious mind sees the world extracted from the world of the unconscious. There is an arrow of intentionality (Husserl 2012, 2013), which we created ourselves before we became aware of any experiences. Understanding this idea from the Eastern philosophical view opens the door to a new approach towards design.

According to de Saussure (2011), our unconscious mind regards the world in a broad sense. The world is interpreted in various ways by language and delivered to the conscious. Our understanding of the world is a linguistic reality. If we apply it to design, only the thing that can be verbalized (frame) becomes the reality for design. What we can design is only that of the pre-defined world, leaving out what lies outside the frame. This is called the "Frame problem", and is a much-talked about issue in artificial intelligence.

A design approach inspired by the Eastern philosophy gives the design a substance of "nothingness" as "chaos" before language or signs are segmented.

5.4 The Ecological Approach to Design

When people look at objects, they themselves unconsciously notice various values regarding the objects. This is what Gibson argued (2014), calling it "affordance". Conventional user interfaces help to guide operations by attaching the information "that could be pressed" into the boundary between users and artefacts. In the world of VR (virtual reality), there is a well-known system called "navigation data".

In order to walk through VR space, dots and mesh are placed to make the users perceive that they "can walk", and topology data to let them know they are "connected". These are realized with "signs" called programming language.

Mathematical symbols are necessary and useful to organize the thoughts that come up to our consciousness. However, there is a big gap between what we believe are thoughts and diversity in the real world. We must discuss what is needed other than symbols to understand the thoughts of the entire world. The advancement of design depends on surpassing them.

5.4.1 The Position of Primitive Design

Since our unconscious world is connected to our body and environment, the conscious part, inferences and elegant thoughts are only the tip of the iceberg, as shown in the figures above. We, as people, make unconscious interpretations which are somehow passed up to consciousness to become perception. Our unconscious actions cannot be described in language and are difficult to interpret using mathematical logic. The phenomenological approach and the ecological approach have shown us the entrance to and boundaries of the unconscious realm.

To answer the question "What is primitive design?" is not easy. It is as difficult to answer as "What is consciousness?". We have to accept the fact that our perception and "thinking" depend on our body. It is our body that determines how we interact with or regard the world. We are not a machine independent of the world but spatial existence regulated by the body–world relationship. Furthermore, the relationship includes a spatial world containing our internal or subjective world. We, who live in the spatial world, are also a temporal existence. The temporal existence is composed of a somatic, physical and pan-space existence trying to live "here and now", and a super-temporal existence trying to go beyond "here and now". In order to achieve an ideal design, we have to construct a fundamental methodology by exploring modes of existence in the world of the deeper mind. It is expected that through repetition of the attempt, we can achieve true universal design which connects design and the realm of unconsciousness. So far, only a few discussions have occurred concerning the approach to the deeper mind in phenomenology and ecology alike. Buddhist philosophy and Eastern thought will give us a clue.

Primitive design is deployed based on Yuishiki/Vijñapti-mātratā theory. The theory argues that "Everything arises from people". It takes the view that nothing exists but one's own mind. All existence is born from Alaya-consciousness to show people various things. It can be said that Yuisiki/Vijñapti-mātratā theory is a model where the world (objective) and inner mind (subjective) are connected. We, people, do not completely separate subject from object. The subject is made up on the basis of its relationship with various objects. Human understanding is also dependent on this relationship (Lakoff and Johnson 2008). We make an action towards an object with a certain degree of preconception. If the object turns out to be what we expected, we continue the action. We are not conscious of the action at this time. For example, imagine a door. If it is the door of the house you live in, you will open and close it by turning the knob in the right direction with the right amount of force without even thinking about it. This is an example often discussed in phenomenology. The smaller the difference between anticipation and reality is, the better united oneself and the world are, creating a harmonious natural flow.

Here, a question arises; what is a "thing"? Designers design "things". Then what are the "things" to design? For example, imagine there is a doorknob made of stainless steel in front of you. Designers have designed a beautiful stainless-steel doorknob with enhanced functionality. Will people always perceive it as a doorknob? Does a doorknob always have the fundamental characteristics with which anyone can perceive it as a doorknob? Not necessarily so, according to Yuishiki/Vijñapti-mātratā theory. A doorknob is a doorknob because we open the door by turning it. Sometimes, it can function as a hook to hang a bag or hanger on. The beautiful stainless-steel thing becomes a doorknob the moment we turn it to open the door. It is not the thing itself that determines the nature, but the action applied to it. A beautiful stainless-steel object can be a doorknob and a hook, depending on the relation between it and people.

This is called "dependent origination (pratītya-samutpāda)" in Buddhism. This is also true in regard to "oneself". There are no grounds for "one being oneself". The existence of oneself emerges in relation to the other existences, and what is more, without him/her being aware of it. Just as the existence of oneself depends on the relations with others and the world, design should be something that emerges from the relationship between people and the environment.

5.4.2 Natural Flow of Action

The body is an image of oneself. Even when we are in abstract thought, the core which is the abstracted body is supposed to be the subject. This is called "image schema" in cognitive science (Lakoff and Johnson 2008). In spite of our perfect existence and creativeness, we people produce numerous imaginary concepts, and we push ourselves into them and suffer. Our reason seems, on the contrary, to inconvenience us. What should we do to get out of this inconvenience that ties us up? We create concepts that are not there but believe in their existence. This false belief turned to "ideology" or "isms" that caused conflicts. If this is the mainstream of our time, what should we do to transcend it?

Eastern philosophy preaches that the world has an "order" that runs through it, and that the flow is on the side of the world. There is no concept or intelligence on the side of the individual self. Giving oneself up to the order on the side of the world achieves a natural flow of action. "Order" (Taoism) is ubiquitous and is the origin of ever-changing things. We must harmonize ourselves with the order; we must harmonize ourselves with the essential flow of the world by relativizing our knowledge.

"Alaya-consciousness" as "chaos" and "nothingness" is the embodiment of the "order". If people force their poor intellect or concepts on the big flow of the world, "chaos" and "order" will be dead. Eastern philosophy warns us that conceptualized intellect may push the natural flow of the order away from us. It tells us: "Human beings by nature are able to behave naturally in the flow by integrating themselves into the world". Eastern philosophy gives us clues as to what specifically should be done and whether we can make use of design in the world, the environment and the natural flow.

As long as people think of themselves as individual existences, they cannot see things in a relative perspective. It is the foundation of Eastern philosophy that we must integrate ourselves with the big flow. The world is not something we should be against, but something we are connected with by one principle. Human beings are a part of the ever-changing wholeness. However, in the West, philosophy is different. For example, Aristotle developed three pillars in his philosophical theories. The first was a category theory to put things into groups, the second was logic, and the third was causality. Mainstream design today is based on the understanding acquired by dividing up the world. The computer has evolved based on the Western view that the properties of intelligence are categorization and inference. Interaction design (HCI) has also evolved in the same way.

Human beings and the physical environment have a neutral relationship. As we mentioned above, it is human actions that determine what a door is, or a hook is. A computer tries to put the world into segments as a sorting machine. However, since people and the environment are, by nature, what Eastern philosophy calls the "ever-changing wholeness", neither computer nor artificial intelligence is able to define this "wholeness" explicitly, at least not completely.

From the Western philosophical point of view, there would be no human intelligence if we eliminated concepts. Intelligence belongs to people, not to the environment. According to this view, it is the human being that has intelligence to perceive the environment. In contrast, Eastern thought considers that intelligence exists in interactions with the world, not on the human side. They repeatedly preach that people can place themselves in the natural flow if they follow the order in the world and allow themselves to harmonize with it.

Design as a stimulus to consumption was born just after the industrial revolution, which started in Britain. The field reflects the attachment of the self and ego in the West. Today, in our information-oriented society, the design of self-attachment shows no sign of slowing down; in fact, quite the contrary. As computers and AI increasingly penetrate our everyday life, we have to make a brand-new start with design, from the perspective of Eastern philosophy. The Western approach, where design, human and environment confront one another, is coming to the end of its tether.

5.5 Conclusion: Consciousness as Where the Self and the World Blend

As the doorknob example shows, how one recognizes a stainless-steel object when he/she sees it may vary depending on individuals—it may be a mere doorknob, or it may be a hook for hanger. If we are "conscious" of how to react once deciding it is a doorknob or a hook in an ontological sense and then take an action after confirmation, we cannot possibly place ourselves in the natural flow. Several possibilities already exist under the unconscious, and one of them goes up to the conscious to achieve the natural flow to determine if it is a doorknob or a hook based on the reality of this very moment.

Information comes in from the limitless world, and the subject decides what to do. When the information is supplied smoothly, the actions and behaviour should flow naturally, too. In order for the information to get in, the subject side should be in a state of nothingness. The emptier the subject is, the more the information flows in, erasing the subject–object relationship. The question is: "How do we achieve that state?". Right now, at this moment, on the subject side, the nested nothingness (emptiness) goes up to the conscious and the object side begins filling the nest moment by moment. The nest starts changing by turns and is filled intermittently. The subject and object have blended. It is a model like this on which artefacts should be made to achieve more human and natural flow.

The human intention to understand the world by dividing it into groups is called "segmentation", which is a view defined by language. People cannot look at the world without the effect of segmentation (Izutsu 1956, 1977, 2007). According to Izutsu, externalized language is the result of segmentation, and there is segmentation occurring before that. For example, prejudices or afflictions work at the deep level of mind before they are expressed by language, which means that segmentation already took place. This is called the "Mana-consciousness" in Buddhism.

The world is not originally segmented, but it is we who see the world segmented with prejudices and afflictions. According to de Saussure (2011), societies force segmentation by languages onto individuals, and then they accept the languages for segmenting the world. People understand the world based on this segmentation. Buddhism transcends segmentation by language and preaches that we take notice of the wholeness as it is, which means to place oneself in the middle of the chaos that seems to be nothing. This is called "emptiness". Faced with the invisible chaos, people living in society consciously segment through prejudices.

Language is the driving force for people to divide the chaos into elements; however, what the West is currently verbalizing seems superficial compared to the chaos. The Western view of design is mainly about its functionality. They question what design functions can do. Even if there is a philosophical discussion on "What is a design?", most of the discussion takes the route of "positivistic" rationalism. While in Eastern thought, the creation of design is the emergence of the intellect of the wholeness, it is language that represents intellect and that is regarded as wisdom in the West, with the focus on its renewability as design.

References

Berkeley G (1999) A treatise concerning the principles of human knowledge. 1710. RS Bear

De Saussure F (2011) Course in general linguistics. Columbia University Press

Freud SSFS (2010) Interpretation of dreams: sigmund Freud's seminal study on psychological dream analysis. Megalodon Entertainment L

Gibson JJ (2014) The ecological approach to visual perception: classic edition. Psychology Press

Husserl E (2013) The idea of phenomenology: a translation of Die Idee Der Phänomenologie Husserliana II, vol 8. Springer Science & Business Media

Husserl E (2012) Ideas: general introduction to pure phenomenology. Routledge

Izutsu T (1956) Language and magic: studies in the magical function of speech, vol 1. The Other Press

Izutsu T (2007) The concept and reality of existence. The other press
Izutsu T (1977) Toward a philosophy of Zen Buddhism
Jung CG (2014) The archetypes and the collective unconscious. Routledge
Lakoff G, Johnson M (2008) Metaphors we live by. University of Chicago press
Lévi-Strauss C (2013) Myth and meaning. Routledge
Scott C (1972) Consciousness and the conditions of consciousness. Rev Metaphys 25(4):625–637. Retrieved May 23, 2020, from www.jstor.org/stable/20126107
Yokoyama K (2002) Yasashii yuishiki. NHK SHUPPAN
Yokoyama K (1979) Yulshikl no tetsugaku. Die welshi-Philosophie), Tokyo

Part III
Design Untamed

In Part III, we present our new design approach in more detail, presenting practical ideas, and concrete examples from our projects. First, we describe exactly how the interaction designer can be reconstructed as a savage or primitive designer, drawing on the theories and foundations presented in Part 2. Next, we outline design processes and methods that are available to carry out primitive interaction design, drawing on both instinct and intellect, including a way of adopting "bricolage" techniques and a way of capturing experiential aspects of interaction through a first-person phenomenological approach. We then present examples of primitive interaction design, allowing the reader to understand the processes applied in different contexts and the practical results.

Chapter 6
The Designer as Savage

Nostromo woke up from a fourteen hours' sleep, and arose full length from his lair in the long grass. He stood knee-deep amongst the whispering undulations of the green blades with the lost air of a man just born into the world. Handsome, robust, and supple, he threw back his head, flung his arms open, and stretched himself with a slow twist of the waist and a leisurely growling yawn of white teeth, as natural and free from evil in the moment of waking as a magnificent and unconscious wild beast. Then, in the suddenly steadied glance fixed upon nothing from under a thoughtful frown, appeared the man.
Joseph Conrad, *Nostromo* (1904)

Abstract The savage mind can be described as the thoughts of "primitive people" without writing. They desire to understand the world around them, its nature, and their society. They are thinkers and also handymen, using so-called *bricolage*, rather disinterested thinking and intellectual reasoning as a philosopher does, and to some extent a scientist. The term *bricolage* has also been used and discussed in many other fields, including anthropology, philosophy, critical theory, education, computer science and business. In this chapter, we attempt to identify design's role neither as an economically viable tool, nor as carried out by conventional mainstream designers. We examine the significance of "design as bricolage" and explore just how bricolage can provide an alternative for new ways of approach to design and to using technology. Further, we argue for mythical thinking as an alternative creative mindset, as opposed to cultivated systematic thought that systematically proceeds from goals to means.

6.1 Introduction

As we have seen, the savage mind can be described as that of "primitive" people without writing. They desire to understand the world around them, its nature and society. They are thinkers and also handymen, using so-called *bricolage*, rather disinterested thinking and intellectual reasoning as a philosopher does, and to some extent a scientist. The term *bricolage* has also been used and discussed in many other fields,

© Springer Nature Switzerland AG 2020

K. Hoshi and J. Waterworth, *Primitive Interaction Design*, Human–Computer Interaction Series,
https://doi.org/10.1007/978-3-030-42954-6_6

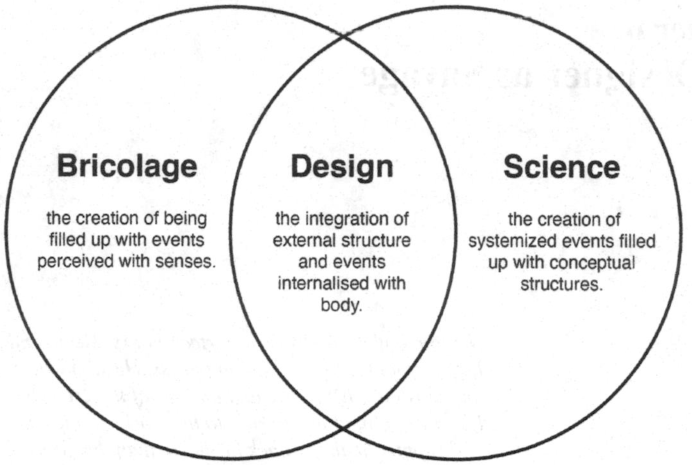

Fig. 6.1 Bricolage, science and design

including anthropology, philosophy, critical theory, education, computer science and business (e.g. Louridas 1999; Markham 2017; Vallgaarda and Fernaeus 2015).

Bricolage can be described as the creation of being, filled up with events and perceived with the senses. On the other hand, science can be seen as the creation of systemized events, filled up with conceptual structure. Primitive design is in the integration of the two. Primitive designers create a structure out of the integration of external structure and events internalized with the body (Fig. 6.1).

In this chapter, we attempt to identify design's role neither as an economically viable tool, nor as carried out by conventional mainstream designers. We examine the significance of "design as bricolage" and explore just how bricolage can provide an alternative for new ways of approaching design and of using technology. Further, we argue for mythical thinking as an alternative creative mindset, as opposed to *cultivated* systematic *thought* that systematically proceeds from goals to means.

By definition, humans design and use tools. In this process, humans are redesigned by their tools. As an example, consider early tool designs. Many archaeologists and anthropologists have argued that teardrop-shaped stone tools in the stone age were designed intellectually to achieve balance and perfection, and they were used as hand tools to make a better hand (Prestwich 1860; Gamble and Kruszynsky 2009; Colomina and Wigley 2016). According to these authors, the human hand is uniquely adapted to make and use tools; the inherited structure of the body has evolved through its technological extensions. The shape of the pieces of stone used for such tools reveals a regularity that implies design, foresight and an intelligent purpose. Their tactile qualities, such as durability, hardness, weight and texture, would have been a determining medium for activating mankind towards the use of their hands. These sensory experiences stimulated their hands and minds and became the driving force of the stone age.

Some scientists and modernists would claim that there is an immense difference between today's humans and these ancient (primitive) people. However, the activities of the latter show intellect and logical reasoning, and the historical difference is only one of degree. In ancient burial grounds, geometric engraving and ornamental beads discovered in Africa and the Middle East show that human creativity does not simply mean the ability to make and use tools. Colomina and Wigley (2016) suggest that ornaments and necklaces dating from between 135,000 and 120,000 BC were used to generate and share information, not just as attractive displays. This is an early example of the human ability to externalize thoughts in symbolic forms used as communication media.

6.2 Primitive Interaction Design as an Attitude

To meet its challenges, primitive design focuses on three main dimensions of the designer and the design process: attitude, understanding and interaction.

The primitive design method places *design attitude* at the core of the interaction design process along with *ways of understanding* (observation and analysis) and *interaction space* (design and prototypical synthesis)—see Fig. 6.2.

Early human artefacts such as shaped stones, ornaments and necklaces were designed in ways that took them beyond material function. They were shared between groups and even between generations in a process that involved tacitly shared knowledge as part of the collective social unconsciousness of early societies. Taking account of this, the designer as savage is guided by a sense of values underlying such a process, such as *grace*, *conscientiousness*, *accuracy* and *simplicity* through minor variations

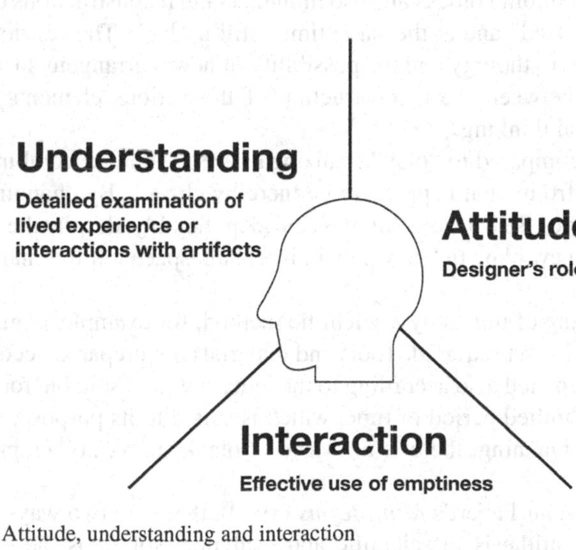

Fig. 6.2 Attitude, understanding and interaction

and improvisation, which can also be described as creating solutions for a problem to be solved out of immediately available found objects.

6.2.1 Designer as Handyman

Bricolage (handiwork) is a concept presented by Levi-Strauss in his book *The Savage Mind* (1966). He was surprised when he learned that the behaviours and thoughts of non-Western indigenous people, who were looked down as simple and crude "savages" from the standpoint of modern Western scientific thinking, were actually based on the unique system classifying and ordering natural phenomena, flora and fauna, and introduced it to the world.

This behavioural thinking style, which has a mythical/magical character, is called "concrete science", as a science that is in no way inferior to modern science. Levi-Strauss describes its form as "bricolage".

The French verb "bricoler" is a word which stands for "to do DIY", In other words, bricolage refers to the act of making things using the tools and materials that are "on hand" and available on the spot, which are not deliberately prepared.

The person who is engaged in this work is called a "bricoleur" (handyman). A bricoleur creates things using ready-made materials and tools, but each "ready-made" thing has its own unique origin (history), and due to the intervention of things such as the evolution of the purpose of use and the roles the things originally had, as well as the deformation which arose during the process of appropriation, the choices of the bricoleurs who construct those groups of materials are limited. Therefore, bricoleurs are required to have a higher level of creativity.

The mythological building blocks are also limited, being reconstructions of things which were "already used" and at the same time "still usable". The restrictions on usage and meaning in mythology and the possibility of new rearrangements demonstrate the similarity between the reconstruction of the various elements used in bricolage and mythical thinking.

Bricolage can be compared to "play" (Huizinga 1938). Children combine materials and create play from what happens to be there by chance. By changing some of the existing play rules (structure), children can adapt flexibly, despite the fact that they are improvising new play. In "play", there is a blank space left for changes and new creations.

In the manufacturing of things by a scientific method, for example, engineering, a blueprint (concept) is first required. Tools and materials are prepared according to the blueprint and completed also according to the blueprint. It is suitable for making the same thing for a limited period of time, which is suited to its purpose, which is called "plan". In the planning, there is no waste or blank space, no "emptiness or Ma".

According to Seymour Papert's *Mindstorms* (1980), there are two ways to solve the problem. As an antithesis to scientific and analytical solutions, he describes problem-solving and learning through challenges, trials and play, which he represents as bricolage. If engineering design or systems design is placed in the "centre", then "play" will be in the "periphery". The vitality and ambiguity of the "periphery" should be the driving force for the stimulation of the borders of the "centre", but design became a servant to system science, engineering and business success, and the original vitality of design has been lost. A design that is out of balance requires "play". It must be brought back to Bricolage!

How do we redefine interaction design as **play** instead of **plan**?

6.2.2 The Trickster-Like Nature of Playing with Design

Since ancient times, humankind has always been entertaining. It's just that the way of playing was one which was in line with their culture and the history of the time. However, it is a big mistake to emphasize only the economic value obtained from the action of play. According to the words of Friedrich Schiller (a German poet of the nineteenth century), "People play only when they are human in the sense of the word, and when they are playing, they are truly human".

"Homo ludens (Huizinga 1938)" is an important basic piece of literature for thinking about the richness of culture and the alternative direction of design, after getting out of the dead end of modern rational society centred on the human perspective of "Homo sapiens (man of reason)" that emphasizes "hard work" and "efficiency", and eliminates any "play" and "surplus". If we compare it to the relationship between the centre and the periphery, rationalistic diligence and efficiency are the "centre", and "play" and "surplus" are driven to the periphery. For example, in medieval Europe, a serious and official church, feudal lords, official culture in the form of national worship and ceremonies, carnival-type square festivals, individual comedic rituals, ceremonies, clowns and travel performers and the like were said to be "informal culture".

Clearly, design was not born out of necessity. It was born of surplus, play and culture. According to Harvard Spencer, play is a divergence of "surplus energy", and if we replace play with design, "design = surplus energy". Design does not exist only in highly developed civilizations. Humankind has not lived for tens of thousands of years driven only by mere need. It's not true that ancients and the Savages didn't play. Their livelihood itself was play, and Huizinga (1938) asserted that, "Human beings are beings that play", that is, Homo ludens, and that play was not born from culture, but culture itself was born and developed as "play" in the first place.

Huizinga conceptualized "play" in a clear way for the first time, and Caillois (2006) approached play in the form of inheriting this research and classifying it according to an original framework. The achievements of these two people in play theory are very large. Of particular importance to Caillois' theory of play is the classification of play and the theory of civilization that sees society using that classification.

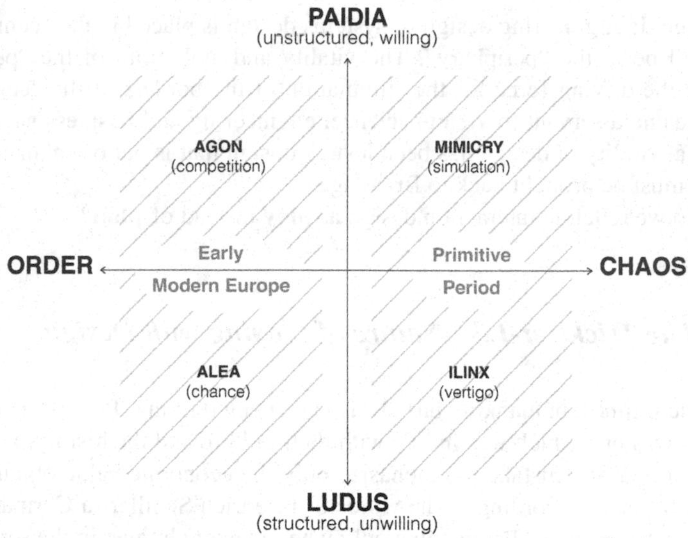

Fig. 6.3 Dimensions of play

Caillois proposed a method to classify play from a unique perspective and attempted what should be called a "taxonomy of play". It looks like this: The horizontal axis is Order calculation/rule ← → Chaos disorder/escape from rule, and the vertical axis is Paidia play/will ← → Ludus martial arts, match/escape from desire. You can see the quadrant where the horizontal axis and the vertical axis intersect (Fig. 6.3).

In each of these quadrants are placed Agon (meaning "competition/match" in Greek), Alea (meaning "luck/bet" in Latin), Mimicry (meaning "imitation/mimesis/copying" in English) and Ilinx (meaning "vertigo" in Greek) (Fig. 6.3). Not all, but most of the world's play is divided into these four quadrants. For example, almost all sports are categorized as Agon; lottery, casino, horse racing as Alea; carnivals, plays and movies as Mimicry; and those with vertigo, screaming machines and merry-go-round as Ilinx.

Caillois further argued that the four quadrants of this play could be used to divide our society into a computational society and a chaotic society (Fig. 6.3). In the computational world, Agon (competitions) and Alea (luck) play an important role in seeking absolutely fair and mathematically equal opportunities through human skills and abilities, and chance and luck. On the other hand, a chaotic society is a society in which mimicry (imitation) and Ilinx (vertigo) are ruled by masks and possessions. Many of the savage societies of Australia and Africa, and the Native American societies are "chaotic societies" characterized by Mimicry (simulation) ← → Ilinx (vertigo), while ancient Rome and modern European societies are "computation (plan) societies" characterized by Agon (competition) ← → Alea (luck). Caillois concluded that: The so-called "road to civilization" is to eliminate the advantage of the combination of Ilinx and Mimicry little by little, and instead place the Agon = Alea pair, the pair of competition and luck, at the top of social relations.

In the process of progressing from undeveloped to civilized, elements of Mimicry and Ilinx in society receded, and elements of Agon and Alea have strongly dominated since the Industrial Revolution. We can get away with spending only a small amount of time on mere survival, there is enough food, lifespans have increased, and we should be able to store "surplus energy". In the information-oriented society, a society that transcends space and time will be built, and the extra use of energy will be devoted to the more intangible Agon and Alea.

However, it is doubtful that the "surplus energy" is being effectively and healthily dissipated. By eliminating the surplus, design, which should naturally have been there, became a target. "Play" has the energy to seek freedom. It is difficult to push the ability to disperse the power that is not utilized in life into the framework of rationality.

6.3 Designer Interaction (Effective Use of Emptiness)

"Space" is written as "間" in Japanese, which is pronounced as "*aida*" or "*ma*". Like the word "space", there are a huge number of common daily words created from "間" in Japanese. This shows how Japanese people continuously perceive "space" unconsciously.

For instance, the word "time (*jikan*)" is made up of two kanji characters "time" and "space" that may be literally interpreted as "space" between points in time. In Japanese, "on time" and "not on time" are said as "match the *ma*" and "not match the *ma*" as concrete illustrations of the Japanese people's perception of "space". The word "human (*ningen*)" also includes the character for "space". If individuals perceive the space between "times", their perception of humans is not individuals but the connections between those individuals, and they are called "human" when they understand such connections.

"Space (*kukan* 空間)" is written as space between emptiness, based on traditional sensations of space between pillars or between walls. The setting of these spatial elements is called "floor plan (*madori*間取り)", which also contains the character "space". "Floor plan (*madori*間取り)" does not merely refer to the size of a house but also literally, "take up space (*aidadori*)". We need space for objects, tools and things, and thus the term "*madori*" (taking up space). Space has the power to have control over objects and tools. In the rooms of a Garando temple, tools are brought in one by one and the space comes to life. When we hang up a scroll or place a vase or an incense burner in the corner, it becomes a "space", a space between emptiness. Japanese people perceive such space in between, and thus, they understand space. It is also important to establish space between a human and tools, as that space is linked to human (*ningen*人間), time (*jikan*時間) and space (*kukan*空間). The creation and perception of the relationship between tools, the relationship between humans, the relationship between points in time when handling tools, and the relationship between tools, humans and space are the "illustration of emptiness" and constitute instinct-like interaction. The fact that humans exist in time is the sharing of "*ma*" with others. Communication is not the exchange of objects or words, but indeed the sharing of "*ma*".

In this way, tools have the power to create space and can make space itself a tool. Some tools come with their own internal space: containers like a box, vase, jar, pot, bowl, dish or tray have spaces both open and closed. When we focus on these internal spaces, space becomes mobile. Cars, ships, aircraft and spaceships are examples of space made to be a tool to serve specific goals, as capsules used as space tools into which other tools are brought.

As mentioned, the creation and perception of the relationships between tools, humans and points in time when handling tools, as well as the relationship between tools, humans and space are the illustration of emptiness and instinct-like interactions. We would like to have a closer look at what is meant by the "relationship" between bodies, tools and space.

Space becomes a space when it has tools, and tools can be space, too. Tools are created by humans with their thoughts, bodies and limbs. Our bodies contain essential organs like hands, feet, eyes, ears, the nose and the mouth that act as tools. We may regard the birth of tools as external extensions of the organs of our bodies.

Hands play an important role in the "relationship" between the body and tools. It is apparent that the functional diversity of hands inspired the invention of many tools. For example, hands can push, hit, slap, rub, pick, grip, press and grasp; hand movements are always versatile and precise. Hands can also measure temperature, length, smoothness and the like. Hands can also count and point. Hands can be playful, like in a game of rock–paper–scissors. Hands are communication tools used in gestures and when we touch or wave them. Sign language using hands has been developed as a substitute for verbal language, and it keeps on changing and improving.

The primitive function of hands is to grip and grasp, which are vitally important. The versatility of hands comes in the hundreds and thousands of functions they can perform. Hoes, sickles and swords encouraged the exploration of the unlimited possibilities for the evolution of tools. Furthermore, the training of the skills, techniques and abilities of hands has inspired the deepening of the performance of tools. Thus, the evolution of the relationship between hands and tools is essential for tools.

Human hands and feet have different forms, while their fundamental structures are the same. All limbs come with five fingers/toes, but feet are not as flexible as hands. Feet are developed to support and balance our body in each step when we walk. Still, the structure of feet is the same as that of hands, and feet can also become hands if we train them, People who lost their hands can draw and write with their feet, recovering the functions in their lower limbs.

In the age when humans made their own tools, they often utilized all four limbs to craft the tools while sitting on the ground and holding the tool with their feet. In traditional Japanese Zori sandals, there is a material separating the big toe and the pointer toe. Japanese people could walk extremely long distances, thanks to this great footwear that successfully harnessed the potential of human feet without adding unnecessary constraints. Traditional Japanese Tabi socks that also separate the big toe with the other toes enabled human feet to work like hands. Despite there being more specialized shoes nowadays, professional Japanese craftspeople still prefer working barefoot or with just Tabi socks.

Hands are also like sensors. They sense temperature in our daily life. Japanese teacups are made with no handle so we can feel the temperature of the tea when we hold the cup in our hands. With experience, hands can distinguish the optimal temperature for the most delicious tea. Hands help us make tools, and tools can do more than hands do. Tools were born to foster the potential of our hands. Machines can work well because there are hands there to help. In factories, machines function under workers' operations. Machines work when workers install bits, drills, blades and nails where they perform the task. Blades deteriorate, but we can reform them and sharpen them by our hands. Hands are crucial to make tools and blades. The Industrial Revolution in Britain successfully ushered in automation, but production quality was worsened without manual work. The Arts and Crafts Movement has pushed back against the low quality stemming from mass production due to the Industrial Revolution, upholding the idea of returning to medieval handicrafts.

Humans evolve alongside the evolution of the use of our hands, which are the basis of human life, as tools. In today's information society, designers utilize the keyboards and mice on their desks, send CAD data files to engineers over the Internet and conduct conference calls. While the ability to read and write is called "literacy", perhaps we should move on and talk about ICT (information–communication technology) literacy. There are no traditional interactions involving the illustration of emptiness in the creation and perception of the relationship between tools, humans, points in time when handling tools, as well as the relationship between tools, humans and space.

6.4 Understanding the World and Designing Man-Made Objects

6.4.1 Tools that Embody Collective Unconsciousness

In the era when tools were born, the wishes of the ancient people became fiction and then turned into tools. Stones became hammers and knives. Stone blades were born from fictional images, and the first earthenware was undoubtedly created by the power of fiction. Fiction usually means "something created to look like fact but made up". However, if such fictional images are not strong enough, people would give up, and those images would not be realized through tools. However, ancient people worked extremely hard and invented a huge number of tools in an environment full of constraints. Their power to imagine fictional objects was fascinating. We should salute the power of imagination of ancient and primitive people who created knives and earthenware. With such power, tools were given lives and souls, and they even allowed humans to communicate with gods. Tools help unite the people who share them and strengthen their collective mindset. Considering this, some say tools embody collective unconsciousness. Compared with the scientific qualities of tools, their figurative and symbolic power is much more freeing and compelling. They pass messages to humans, so it is also believed that tools contributed to resolving contradictions faced by groups of humans, as is said in myths.

Jomon ornamental pottery was a ritual instrument that brought prayers to gods, and the blade became one of the three holy instruments representing the heavenly gods later in Japan. In a fictional form, tools become spiritual media. Tools become more sophisticated as they embrace words and carry meaning.

People understand that tools are spiritual crystals of the human image in the virtual, fictional world. This is the essence of humans and animals who create tools. Humans aim to realize the fictions in their internal world by creating and living with tools. This is a process of creating fictional frameworks. In other words, tools are the infrastructure for fiction and imagination.

6.4.2 Structuring the Subjective World Through Design

Colomina and Wigley (2017) actively borrow knowledge from evolutionary biology, anthropology, archaeology and neuroscience to present the idea that humans have been creating tools and using them to proactively design and redesign themselves for hundreds of years. The generalization of all historical and modern theories of design has made modern humans recognize that design contributes to our lives by superseding products and architecture and making everything in this world a creation. They also strongly believe that designs and man-made objects hundreds of years ago shaped the humans of that era. At their core, tools are extensions of humans. We can also interpret tools as supplements for humans that have existed since we first came into existence. Supplements have been understood as artificial, man-made objects that compensate for our weaknesses or losses in our physical functions, but when we try perceiving them instead as extensions of our understanding and scope of movement, the tools made hundreds of years ago were all supplements.

Man-made objects are supplements, and they are tools to extend human ability. Stones, the first tools of humankind, were one of these supplements. According to neuroscientific theories, our brain can fine-tune and update neural circuits when we use supplements and man-made objects. That means humans are changing—they are trying to understand the world through their tools, or we can even assert that man-made objects themselves are indeed representations of our thoughts. Those tools used by primitive and ancient people give us a glimpse into their worldviews. When a man-made object embodies thoughts, the worldview of its user is simultaneously updated. What we make and design helps us understand the world in a boarder sense.

This cycle has been repeating for hundreds of years. Humans make tools to understand the world, think of the fictional and explore new worlds, and they eventually change themselves. Tools always come with the realization of the fictional. If we switch the invention of tools with the design of tools, we can see design as the

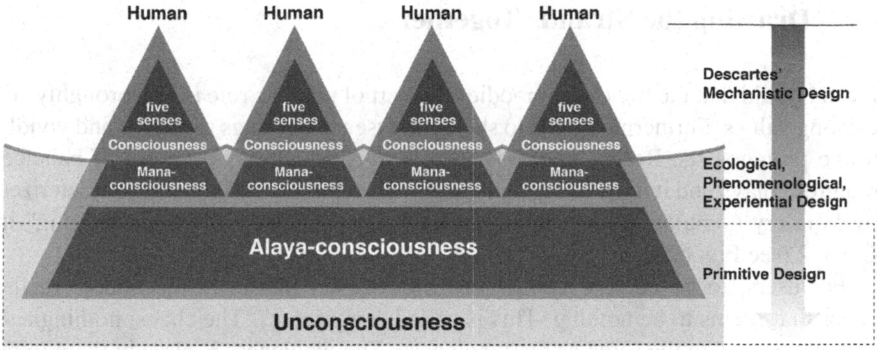

Fig. 6.4 Primitive design in relation to consciousness and the collective unconscious

structure of a subjective world (the structure of the deep spirit and sensations in a human's internal world). We can imagine that ancient and primitive people shared tools, but they were not merely sharing tools. They were sharing their subjective worlds encapsulated in those tools, as media, without the limitations of time. This interaction is a sharing of "space" in the subjective world. Even when tools grow old, the human thoughts embedded in shared tools like stones can still be passed down across generations to the modern world.

Figure 6.4 shows an illustration of primitive design in relation to consciousness and the collective unconscious of Carl Jung. According to the perspectives of phonemic ontology, ecological psychology (affordance) and cognitive semantics (metaphor), our understanding of the world of our sensations is mainly unconscious. While this theory has been actively applied to the aspect of design to improve design, our primitive design goes one step further in an attempt to focus on its application to design on a deeper level of collective unconsciousness. A true universal design is not limited by any individual thoughts, and we must place our focus beyond the collective consciousness of any group or society and on to another level.

Collective unconsciousness is constructed from a common archetype possessed by all humans (a human's original form). Carl Gustav Jung contended that a common symbolism exists on the deep level of a human's unconsciousness based on his research of religious symbols, myths, folklore, literature and arts. We are convinced that primitive interaction design, our true human-centred design, exists because of our understanding of this area. In the theory of subjective existence, this touches on the concept of consciousness forming the base of all human existence (Fig. 6.4).

6.5 Drawing the Strands Together

It can be said that the trickster embodies the part of play. Its role is to thoroughly stir existing values. Furthermore, it is to show the essence of things stealthily and vividly to the protagonists. Recent market-driven design, which has been out of balance, requires "play" and it must be brought back to the chaotic world that is characterized by Mimicry (simulation) ← → Ilinx (vertigo), which we call "back to being" in Chap. 2 (see Fig. 6.5).

For users, to go back to being is to find oneself placed in the middle of the chaos that seems to be nothing. This is called "emptiness". The chaos, nothingness and emptiness are the same as the wholeness. The wholeness is already there to be dug out. Giving oneself up to being achieves a natural flow of action. They harmonize themselves with the essential flow of the chaos by relativizing their knowledge. If users force their intellect or concepts on the entire flow, it is impossible for them to behave naturally in the flow by integrating themselves into the world. Eastern philosophy warns us that conceptualized intellect may push the natural flow of action away from us.

When we fully utilize a tool, our body becomes a tool as well. This has been true since the origin of all tools. Humans cannot make new tools until they fully utilize their body as a tool. That was, in fact, the only thing that primitive and ancient people could do. In other words, our body must be fully complete as a tool itself before we can use any tools. Understanding the relationship between tools and human bodies

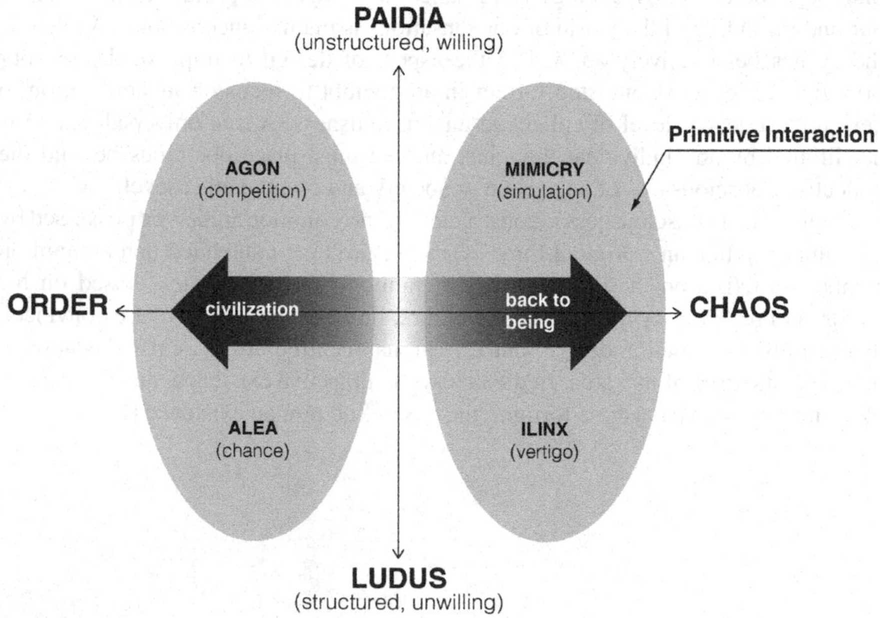

Fig. 6.5 From order to chaos, from civilisation back to being

enhances both. In this sense, digital space should be a medium that transforms manual work into digital tools.

Virtual space is also used as a tool for particular purposes, and it is also a tool space having perceptual encapsulation. Here, people and tools transcend time and space and behave as an integrated medium of expression for the design of new tools. Tools are made into time and space, so humans, tools and space are all integrated. It is an "illustration of emptiness" in virtual space. Primitive interaction can be interpreted as a creative "illustration of emptiness" in the digital space as a tool.

Consider design as an opportunity to have a dependent origination relationship with the world.

- Emptiness: Neither existence nor non-existence
- Non-ipseity: Everything is a dependent origin existence
- Dependent origination: Everything is made up based on relationships

When we incorporate "dependent origination, non-ipseity and emptiness" into design, design can be existent and not existent (neither existence nor non-existence). Design is something to be generated. All we need is a design for an excuse for the inner flow of the self and the external flow from the world to co-create. That means discussing design from the viewpoint of "dependent origination, non-ipseity and emptiness". In short, design as a place to generate behaviour and perception, namely, design as "emptiness". Nothing exists at the heart of design. However, design is made up on the relationship with everything (dependent origination). We should reconstruct design as the "place where everything meets", not as a fixed entity (non-ipseity).

The "place where everything meets" is, according to the dependent origination idea, the place for co-creation where design produces reality. It is not only information about processing that comes into the "place", but also all the elements that form oneself in relation with the world, and their influences. All phenomena concerning the relationship with materialistic and physical elements, with circumstances, and with oneself are this "place", and this "place" is nothing but design. What influences the design "place" might be such ambient information as climate, sunset or breeze. It could be the tweet of a bird. There may be a "place" where these elements are intertwined at one time. If various material and informational elements in the world exist in relation to oneself, and if design exists in relation to existence, the "place" of design arises in every existence.

References

Caillois R (2006) The definition of play and the classification of games. Game Design Reader: A Rules Play Anthol 122

Colomina B, Wigley M (2016) Are we human? Notes on an archaeology of design. Lars Müller Publishers, Zürich, Switzerland

Gamble C, Kruszynski R (2009) John Evans, Joseph Prestwich and the stone that shattered the time barrier. Antiquity 83(320):461–475

Huizinga J (1938) Homo ludens. Editora Perspectiva SA

Levi-Strauss C (1966) The savage mind. University of Chicago Press

Louridas P (1999) Design as bricolage: anthropology meets design thinking. Des Stud 20(6):517–535

Markham A (2017) Select Page Bricolage: A keyword in remix studies.

Prestwich J (1860) XVII. On the occurrence of flint-implements, associated with the remains of animals of extinct species in beds of a late geological period, in France at Amiens and Abbeville, and in England at Hoxne. Philos Trans R Soc Lond 150:277–317

Seymour P (1980) Mindstorms: children, computers and powerful ideas. Basic Book, New York

Vallgaarda A, Fernaeus Y (2015) Interaction design as a bricolage practice. In: Proceedings of the ninth international conference on tangible, embedded, and embodied interaction, pp 173–180

Chapter 7
Primitive Interaction Design: Methods

Abstract In this chapter, we sketch out the practicalities of the primitive approach to designing interactive systems. We lay out methods for practices that incorporate key principles, which have been presented in earlier chapters. These methods include the capturing of experiences by applying interpretive phenomenological analysis; techniques for maintaining necessary emptiness for this; how to actively promote doing as being, unconscious design and interaction consequences; and how to approach design as bricolage, for example using morphogenetic prototyping.

7.1 Introduction

In this chapter, we sketch out the practicalities of the primitive approach to designing interactive systems. We lay out the process and methods for practices that incorporate the following key principles presented in earlier chapters:

- Capturing experiences by applying interpretive phenomenological analysis
- Techniques for maintaining necessary emptiness
- Actively promoting doing as being, unconscious design and interaction consequences
- Approaching design as bricolage, for example using morphogenetic prototyping

The methods described are suitable for understanding the shape and the details of lived human experiences of people with artefacts. Our brief earlier review of anthropological, archaeological and design aspects of primitive people has shown that the behaviour of making stone tools, designing tools and designing interactions must trigger the necessary mindfulness to improve the doing (through interaction) in designing utilitarian aesthetics. People's creative urges are evoked by interacting with tools (artefacts), and humans are altered by their interactions with technology. Interaction and humans produce each other socially, culturally and as-if physically. Put another way, interactive artefacts are not mere extensions of the human body; they are part of the constitution of the body necessary to be human in today's external reality.

© Springer Nature Switzerland AG 2020

K. Hoshi and J. Waterworth, *Primitive Interaction Design*,
Human–Computer Interaction Series,
https://doi.org/10.1007/978-3-030-42954-6_7

Primitive interaction design is the act of externalization, not just knowledge in the brain. It helps to evoke a new sense of the interior, for without an outside there can be no inside. Artefact, body and mind are inseparable. Thinking should not be regarded as just a mindset in your head. Thoughts are partly the result of the gestures of externalization that potentially also invite new modes of thought. Thoughts only occur in the interaction between inside and outside.

Interpretive phenomenological analysis is presented as a way of understanding key experiential aspects of user intentions and activities as well as the interactions that may support (or hinder) them. We discuss how the primitive approach to design and phenomenological analysis complement each other, for example, showing how the method can help unveil meanings concealed behind human unconscious behaviours, as well as how observing and discussing interactions can clarify design expectations.

Drawing on insights derived from our phenomenological analysis method, morphogenetic prototyping (McGinley et al. 2016) is introduced as a practical primitive design method for actively exploring interaction possibilities. It arose from the incorporation of free movement interaction techniques into practical design work, as an alternative to the usual process based on the use of conventional user interface tools and design packages. In the application of this method, a particular kind of conceptual space is created, one in which the designer can easily draw parallels between, for example, architecture, biology and everyday life. This can be used to generate a field of interaction objects and gestures. By mapping the gestures to meanings and functions within the scope of, in this example, architecture and biology, a set of actions for a designed virtual space is created.

7.2 Capturing Experiences by Applying Interpretive Phenomenological Analysis

Phenomenology tells us that we should accept that the world cannot be understood fully by a Cartesian approach and that we should also take more experiential aspects into consideration. Although phenomenology also describes aspects of consciousness that have intent towards objects, there is a world that is difficult to describe and understand. Design may have the potential to contribute to understanding and reconstructing the subjective experiential world as a whole. It may seem possible to understand the world if we leverage big data and frequently use smart algorithms; however, it is still rather difficult. The "world understood by contemplation" was once implemented in artefacts that penetrated our everyday life. But the world that cannot be comprehended by a Cartesian approach has ended up being discarded.

What phenomenology teaches us about design can be summed as follows:

- Understanding the "world" goes beyond an approach to "artefacts that think".
- We need to go beyond understanding of the mechanistic "world" to constructing artefacts integrated with the subjective world consisting of collective intentionality.

- A description of artefacts and the "world" as a whole, by covering not only intentionality towards the environment outside the "self", but also all mental activities including thought, should be our aim.

The objects of intentionality in phenomenology (Husserl 2012) are not only "things" but also experiences concerning the world that contains the things, which includes memories and the subconscious. "All the mental activities including thoughts" as mentioned above contain memories and consciousnesses inside the human mind. However, approaches to this deeper layer are yet to be sufficiently discussed even in phenomenology, although Buddhist philosophy and Eastern thought provide us with clues as discussed earlier.

Phenomenology has been discussed quite extensively in HCI from time to time (for a recent example, see Gunkel 2018) but there are few, if any, clear descriptions about how to go about using phenomenological insights when conducting interaction design. In the context of architectural design, a useful overview by Seamon (2000) brings out some important relevant points. These include two key assumptions of the phenomenological approach that mesh with the approach we are presenting:

- people and the world in which they exist comprise a whole that cannot be usefully divided; and
- what is needed in design is a kind of radical empiricism—one that takes account of what is the case and feeds this back to create new (design) knowledge, but not in the standard ways of the scientific method.

Seamon (2000) also identifies three classes of phenomenological method: (1) first-person phenomenological research; (2) existential–phenomenological research; and (3) hermeneutical- phenomenological research. These correspond to, firstly, the designer reflecting on her own feelings and experiences, perhaps as a way of raising her consciousness of the issues involved in a design; secondly, the designer focusing on experiences in very specific situations or places; and, thirdly, the designer trying to interpret what respondents write or say about an issue, almost as a form of literary interpretation.

Phenomenological enquiry is uniquely sensitive to context and personal experience. In this sense, it does not aim or claim to generate generalizable knowledge. It has much in common with ethnomethodology which looks at the methods people use (hence, the name ethnomethodology—it is not a methodology, but the study of people's methods) in social situations (Garfinkel 1984). Ethnomethodology is primarily descriptive and is responsible for the development of conversational analysis. This can be used in design as a way of identifying what is going on in people's answers to questions or stories. The primitive interaction designer seeks to intuit what methods people use to achieve their purposes, act out their intentions, in actual places and settings, and what their experience is in doing so.

For the phenomenologically aware designer, a key activity is *intuiting*. As Spiegelberg (1982) puts it, intuiting: "is one of the most demanding operations, which requires utter concentration on the object intuited without being absorbed in it to the point of no longer looking critically. Nevertheless, there is little that the beginning phenomenologist can be given by way of precise instructions beyond such metaphoric phrases as 'opening his eyes', 'keeping them open', 'not getting blinded', looking and listening" (Spiegelberg 1982, p. 682). The designer needs to approach a situation openly and modestly, assuming he/she doesn't understand a situation until he/she has immersed himself/herself in it. The designer cannot base his/her design work on second-hand knowledge, but must find out for himself/herself, without prior assumptions. The thing or place should be studied without a theory of what it is or how it works. Intense, open-minded exposure to the object is needed, allowing impressions to coalesce into insights.

Maintaining this open and modest attitude, some of the strategies that can be used include the following:

- Talking to people, preferably in situ, in a way that brings out their experiences, the experiential aspects of the phenomenon. This might be in the form of question and answer interviews, but the designer must be sensitive to the interviewee and "go with the flow" of their answers.
- Gathering grounded stories, narratives of the way people experience a situation—such as using an artefact in practice—emphasizing interest in personal experiences in context.
- Observing people in context.
- Acting out situations in 3D space contexts.
- Observing others act out situations in 3D space contexts.

Data richness and openness of the designer are key to the success of this process. The designer approaches a design situation with an open mind, acknowledging that he/she does not understand the situation but wants to. The designer exposes himself/herself to the data, in one form or another, as much of it as possible, without imposing form on it. During this immersion process, it is essential that he/she maintains the necessary emptiness. Over prolonged exposure, with rich, instance-based information percolating through her unconscious, fragments of understanding are allowed to gradually cohere in consciousness. At some stage, one or more insights emerge, intuited to be meaningful and relevant to the provoking situation. The designer then uses these insights while creating designed forms of and for interaction.

7.3 Techniques for Maintaining Necessary Emptiness

"Emptiness" is the world's true form. Its existence is usually not taken notice of by people. However, it is where every existence arises. The forms of individual existences emerge from there, but the individuals were originally the undivided emptiness, and everything is connected. "Things" are fluid. While everything is related and in motion, at the same time they are in motion as a whole. Nothing is alone. When the aspect of being, which is the origin of every existence, comes to the front, "emptiness" starts functioning as a powerful affirmation principle of existence. "Emptiness" is considered negative in Western philosophy. Reversing the negative into a positive is called "Kotowari (reason)" (Yokoyama 1979).

Primitive interaction design is based on the system of "dependent origination, non-ipseity, and emptiness". By this view, it is the role of design and designers to provide people with room for creating the world embedded with everything from the body, the self, the subjective world, to behaviour, in order for people to exist in the natural flow. Primitive interaction designers should:

- Consider design as an opportunity to have a dependent origination relationship with the world.
- Seek emptiness: Neither existence nor non-existence.
- Remember non-ipseity: Everything is in dependent existence.
- Remember dependent origination: Everything is made up based on relationships.

In Eastern thought, being empty is the state wherein "something is present and absent", which means "neither existence nor non-existence". Being "present" is "existing" as generative existence. Even if it is present, it vanishes voluntarily; therefore, it is "nothing", they preach. In other words, there is no real static existence as we presuppose. In Western thought, things themselves have unique natures or self-identity; this is called "ipseity" (Yokoyama 1979). On the other hand, "emptiness" thought preaches that there is no "ipseity of things". This is called "non-ipseity".

For example, a doorknob does not necessarily have universal ipseity. It can be a hook for hangers and bags. In the subjective world then, the doorknob is a hook. Cognitive science calls this affordance. "Emptiness" thought does not preach that a thing does not exist as it is, but that what we can see at this moment is "seen" based on connections of various elements. This means that our understanding of the world "is based on relationship, and is not independent". The thing has non-ipseity but it looks existent.

When we incorporate "dependent origination, non-ipseity and emptiness" into design, design can be existent and not existent (neither existence nor non-existence). Design is something to be generated. All we need is a design for an excuse for the inner flow of the self and the external flow from the world to co-create. That means discussing design from the viewpoint of "dependent origination, non-ipseity and emptiness". In short, design as a place to generate behaviour and perception, namely, design as "emptiness". Nothing exists at the heart of design. However, design is made up on the relationship with everything (dependent origination). We should reconstruct design as the "place where everything meets", not as a fixed entity.

The "place where everything meets" is, according to the dependent origination idea, the place for co-creation where design produces reality. It is not only information about processing that comes into the "place", but also all the elements that form oneself in relation with the world and their influences. All phenomena concerning the relationship with materialistic and physical elements, with circumstances, and with oneself, are this "place", and this "place" is nothing but design. What influences the design "place" might be climate, sunset or breeze. It could be the tweet of a bird. There may be a "place" where these elements are intertwined at one time. If various material and informational elements in the world exist in relation to oneself, and if design exists in relation to existence, the "place" of design arises in every existence.

Design, then, is a "place". With this perspective, body and mind are not separated but exist in the interaction. Everything is originally based on the relationship of dependent origination and everything influences everything. While creating a design in the world, we should also create a design which is a part of the flow of the world, the environment and the universe. This is similar to the relationship between homeostasis and apoptosis (Dexter 1995). When our self-retaining function is too strong, we become too attached to ourselves and end up suffering. This is called homeostasis. Trying to get out of cultural restraints that immobilize us, we throw ourselves out towards the world and behave as a part of the world's flow. This is apoptosis. Here, unconscious self-preservation movements should be performed smoothly. That is the key. If we take part in the world intentionally and try to control the world, we are enforcing our own world and end up suffering.

The transition back and forth between homeostasis and apoptosis can be seen as a state of unconsciousness. Most humans are largely living in a state of unconsciousness. People limited by unconscious cultural grip are living in their own world, a world, for example, of conceptual categorization, judgment and belief, or a world of the remembered past and the imagined future—an ideological world, not an experiential world. They are absorbing into the internal world of their thoughts and imagination based on their cultural environment. It gives them a sense of the self as existing outside of the present moment (Waterworth et al. 2015). It also produces a sense of separation from the external world and breaks the human natural flow of action that is based on constant activity.

Emptiness is the place where judgements by conceptual thought are suspended and where the world is not divided up. The undivided world itself exists there. Humans divide up the world by "concept" in order to understand it. When this human understanding of relationships by way of conceptual division is removed, "emptiness" emerges. On the other hand, when functioning smoothly, humans act with unconscious motor behaviour, they are attending to the here and now, and have a sense of complete absorption in the external world of the present.

Essentially, humans are supposed to be able to live in this flow, and they should already know it but have forgotten it, which is a state of emptiness. The role of design is not to create a new experience, but to make people realize what they already know. It gives us the awareness that it is already there.

7.4 Actively Promoting Doing as Being, Unconscious Design and Interaction Consequences

The world we see also represents ourselves. It is we that make a subjective world of our own by using information and stimulation from objects. Various contexts come to us; some are cultural, others are social. They are disassembled, understood and reconstructed. They are also ourselves. We are trying to connect to the world in between the conscious and unconscious. On one hand, there is the external consciousness that tries to shape the self by going beyond the world's flow. The other is the unconsciousness that tries to become one with the world's flow. The stream of consciousness is created by placing oneself in the midst of the world's flow. In most circumstances, we let our unconsciousness take the initiative. But from time to time, we consciously place ourselves in the unconscious just like a fish let loose in a clear stream. Even when we read a book, we go back and forth between physical and conceptual experiences, the unconscious and the conscious. We are going back and forth between the world's flow, where our body belongs, and the flow of subjective time—which depends on conscious thought.

Things are persistent. The body lies in the multiplicity of such persistence. The body is always in an uninterrupted, gapless, persistent state. When you try to design an interaction, you tend to assume the attitude of trying to generate it. Rather than generating an interaction, it would be more appropriate to think of it as already occurring. We are always in harmony with the environment. For example, there is a famous experiment called "moving room" (Lee and Aronson 1974). In an environment where the walls and floor are separated, the surrounding walls are suspended by a few millimetres, and the walls are designed to move back and forth. The participant of the experiment enters the room and simply stands upright. When the walls are moved back and forth, the walls and the participant's body move synchronously, of which the participant is not aware. This experiment shows that humans use the walls' persistent information unconsciously. In other words, it shows that humans are unconsciously in harmony with environmental information. We are actively passive and in harmony with the environment. Therefore, in order to design an interaction, it is important to understand the interactions that humans use in their daily lives and to consider that interactions have already been occurring in the persistent state. Designing an interaction is not so much about creating it as it is about coordinating the body, perception and action in the persistent state. The experience is in an unconscious state that does not even make you aware of the coordination.

The existence of an environment that embraces humans and animals is not to be regarded as an illusion created by perception, but as a human–environment or human-world system. People and the environment (world) are not separated but closely connected by perceptions and actions. Actions bring out the value of the environment in real time, where humans and animals perceive possibilities, leading to the next action. In addition to action, when a tool that expands the action intervenes between the person and the environment, the possibility of another dimension is perceived, which leads to another action. Good tools are especially competent to let us perceive this possibility. Environment and sequential perceptions and actions circulate without interruption, which is the true nature of interactions.

Understanding this series of processes is an essential part of interaction design. As Fig. 7.1 (based on Watanabe 2015) shows, the farther the body is from the target object, the more the number of boundaries increases, which makes it more difficult to persistent in this flow, and the harmony with the world is disturbed. As a result,

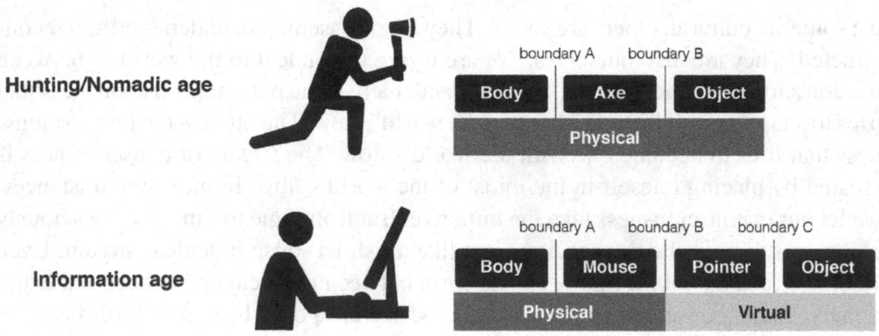

Fig. 7.1 Increase in boundary issues with bodily distancing

Fig. 7.2 Optimal design with no added boundary issues

we move away from "emptiness". People behave in a natural flow, expand the world with tools and embody the "emptiness" when they are in perfect harmony with the environment (Fig. 7.2).

As described in Chap. 5, it is the practice of "everything is already there". The concept of primitive interaction design is that humans excavate what is already there not consciously but in the unconscious state that is shared by the whole.

7.5 Approaching Design as Bricolage in Blended Reality Space

To support primitive interaction design it is necessary to provide materials that evoke our creative impulses, as well as a social space in which to share human creativity beyond time and space. The set of characteristic patterns of collective unconsciousness, such as human attitude, behaviour and aesthetic sense that we have described above, are precisely the resources needed to engage in interaction design as bricolage. Emptiness in this context goes beyond modernism and simplicity, as well as the packaged (restricted structure) design mindset aimed principally at problem-solving.

Interactions should rather be designed as challenges to existing concepts of interaction. This opens up new understandings of what could be interactions and what interaction could be (for). By this view, interaction is not a given need filled up with functionalities. Ambiguity about interaction is what drives new forms of interaction. This involves the effective use of negative space which, through constraint and absence, encourages audiences to make complements, drawing on images from their own experiential knowledge.

Crafted and used by handyman, the stone axe marked the first in a series of major toolmaking advances among early humans. A similar approach is used with a primitively designed tool in blended reality space (Fig. 7.2) to manipulate an artefact or architecture through biology as a means of morphogenetic prototyping, as an interface to enact bricolage. The user perceives the world within an immersive environment and behaves directly with the agile aXe (McGinley et al. 2016), as in everyday unmediated activities. Modelled forms can be meaningfully manipulated, and the consequences of the user's actions are felt in real time. Interactions in the space are not designed to carry out defined utilitarian tasks, but rather as challenges to existing concepts of interaction. This opens up new possibilities for understanding what could be interacted with and how.

When a primitive interaction design space is successfully functioning, designers are freed from conscious thoughts and behave within it using largely unconscious motor behaviour, with a sense of absorption in contextual emptiness, the external world of the present. Instead of the way of planning, they are playing, where they can adapt flexibly despite the fact that they are improvising new play. In "play", there is an empty space left for changes and new creations.

This means that they are attending to the here and now and not to the intricacies of an unnatural design tool. The users in the space behave as if they were both sacred and lewd bricoleurs, re-enacting trickster myths. In Chap. 8, we present morphogenetic prototyping in blended reality space in detail and discuss how unconscious being, myth and emptiness are integrated and embedded into the system.

References

Dexter RM (1995) The role of apoptosis in development, tissue homeostasis and malignancy: death from inside out. Springer Science & Business Media

Garfinkel H (1984) Studies in ethnomethodology. Polity Press, Cambridge

Gunkel DJ (2018) The relational turn: third wave HCI and phenomenology. In: Filimowicz M, Tzankova V (eds) New directions in third wave human-computer interaction: Volume 1—Technologies. Human–computer interaction series. Springer, Cham.

Husserl E (2012) Ideas: general introduction to pure phenomenology. Routledge.

Lee DN, Aronson E (1974) Visual proprioceptive control of standing in human infants. Percept Psychophys 15(3):529–532

McGinley T, Hoshi K, Gruber P, Haddy S, Zavoleas Y, Tan L, Blaiklock D (2016) A katana design experience. In: Intersections in simulation and gaming. Springer, Cham, pp 134–148

Seamon D (2000) A way of seeing people and place: phenomenology in environment-behavior research. In: Wapner S, Demick J, Yamamoto T, Minami H (eds) Theoretical perspectives in environment-behavior research. Plenum, New York, pp 157–178

Spiegelberg H (1982) The phenomenological movement. Martinus Nijhoff, Dordrecht, The Netherlands

Watanabe K (2015) Sukeru dezain. PNN, Tokyo
Waterworth J, Lindh Waterworth E, Riva G, Mantovani F (2015) Presence: form, content and consciousness. In: Immersed in media: telepresence theory, measurement & technology. Springer, New York, pp 35–58. https://doi.org/10.1007/978-3-319-10190-3_3.
Yokoyama K (1979) Yulshikl no tetsugaku. Die welshi-Philosophie, Tokyo

Chapter 8
Primitive Interaction Design Examples

Abstract In this chapter we present two examples of primitive interaction design in action. The first illustrates several of the principles that we have discussed earlier in the book: the use of myth as inspiration, unconscious (embodied) interaction, and designing for specific emotions. In the second, morphogenetic prototyping is introduced as a practical primitive design method for actively exploring interaction possibilities. In the application of this method, a particular kind of conceptual space is created, one in which the designer can easily draw parallels between, for example, architecture, biology and everyday life. This can be used to generate a field of interaction objects and gestures. By mapping the gestures to meanings and functions within the scope of, in this example, architecture and biology, a set of actions for a designed virtual space is created.

8.1 Primitive Interaction Design in Practice

We present two examples of primitive interaction design in practice. The first example—the Exploratorium—draws on several elements of primitive interaction design that we presented in earlier chapters: myth, designing for emotion, unconscious (embodied) interaction and emptiness. This example illustrates the use of primitive design methods in the design process.

In the second example, we demonstrate the use of an axe as an appropriately primitive interaction tool for "bricolage as design" and also as an alternative to traditional CAD and user interface models. Conventional Computer-Aided Design (CAD), with limited screen-based forms of interaction, may not be the most appropriate design experience. We developed a blended reality space where designers can create a design through playful bricolage. It illustrates the dynamic process of design as play.

Increases in computation power have allowed design software tools to become more complex. At the same time, big data and artificial intelligence question the traditional tools of the human designers, which require them to conceptually plan to

© Springer Nature Switzerland AG 2020

K. Hoshi and J. Waterworth, *Primitive Interaction Design*,
Human–Computer Interaction Series,
https://doi.org/10.1007/978-3-030-42954-6_8

design an artefact. In this chapter along with ways of viewing the designer as savage, we suggest that interaction design can be redefined as playing instead of planning.

8.2 The Exploratorium: An Environment for Emotional Self-discovery

The Exploratorium[1] was designed as a virtual environment within which participants can explore a mythical world and the feelings this generates, by means of a form of interaction that maps directly onto the body and requires little conscious thought. It is an environment in which a participant can learn, experience, enhance and understand her feelings better, though interaction. See Fig. 8.1.

The implemented narrative is structural/architectural rather than linear storytelling. What happens there depends on what the participant does by navigation, which is synonymous with interaction. If they don't do move, nothing will happen; or, put another way, their navigation determines the story they experience in this mythical world.

8.2.1 Designing a Mythological World

Many myths and religions include the idea of levels of being, each level being characterized by specific qualities and associated emotions. More specifically, many include the idea of an afterlife, which can be endured or enjoyed after death. The idea of going to a wonderful place—by whatever route—if you have lived successfully, and

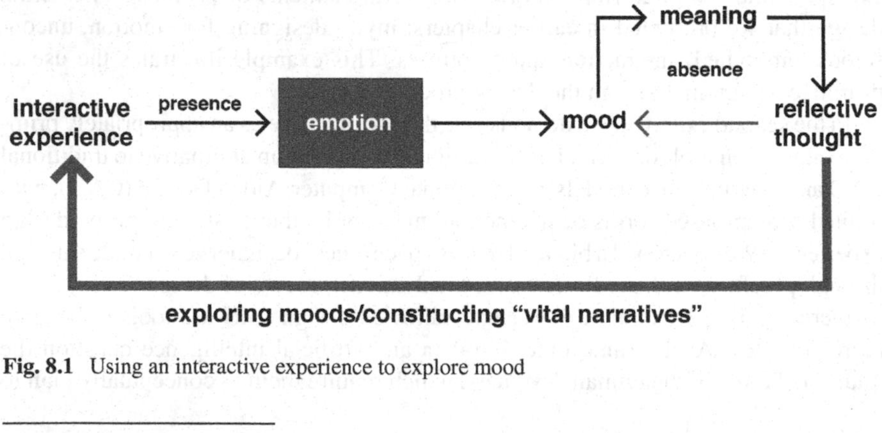

Fig. 8.1 Using an interactive experience to explore mood

[1] The Exploratorium was created by members of the Interactive Institute Tools studio, including Sandra Olsson, Eva Lindh Waterworth, Kalle Jalkanen and Markus Häggqvist, assisted by other partners in the EMMA project, funded by the EU.

a terrible place if you haven't, is of mythic significance in a variety of cultures. We took this myth as the starting point for the Exploratorium. We designed the virtual world as three "zones" arranged vertically, very loosely based on Dante's Divine Comedy version of Christianity: Purgatorio (central zone), Paradiso (top zone) and Inferno (lower zone).

The space is arranged in such a way that it relates metaphorically to mood or feeling state. The idea is that participants can navigate between different zones within the Exploratorium and encounter surroundings that suggest, and even provoke, particular emotional states. In addition to visual features, the Exploratorium contains sound effects and music appropriate to each part.

Upward movement thus suggests improving or lightening mood, whereas downward movement corresponds to deteriorating or darkening mood. The user should be able to move between zones to experience different states, and the method of navigation should emphasize or amplify the changes as well as the degree of control over those changes. The Exploratorium was designed as an environment in which to learn about oneself and one's embodied being.

Different areas of the Exploratorium present different experiences: scary, everyday, or very calm. At the same time, the Exploratorium as a whole is experienced as safe, a self-contained play area. Participants can, if they wish, experience the more challenging parts or remain in the more relaxing ones. They are free to explore the different areas, under their own control.

8.2.2 Unconscious Interaction

It would be possible in principle to navigate in the Exploratorium using a variety of devices, such as joysticks, wands and so on, but the design was more specifically suited to an intimate, embodied style of interaction. We created a new technique the Body Joystick, which uses a vest worn by the participant, and includes sensors for both body orientation and chest expansion in breathing. It was inspired by the powerful immersive artwork Osmose of Char Davies (1998). We adapted her navigation idea by making the vest lightweight and wireless, and we did not use a Head Mounted-Display but rather a large back-projection screen.

The Exploratorium differs from most virtual environments in that it emphasizes the vertical dimension of navigation as well as the horizontal. The participant slips on the vest, and it is fastened across the chest. A small sensor and wire across the front detect expansion and contraction of the chest during intake and expulsion of air while breathing. Breathing in and holding the breath will result in the participant moving up in the virtual space of the Exploratorium. Breathing out and holding will cause the participant to move down. Normal breathing will maintain the participant at a steady vertical position. Movement on the horizontal plane is controlled by balance. If the participant leans forward, he/she will move forward in virtual space; leaning backward results in backward movement. The participant can turn right by leaning to the right, and left by leaning to the left.

This is a very natural and embodied way of interacting, which soon becomes almost unconscious. Participants talk about "floating" or "flying" in the world, about "going in" and "backing out". They don't talk about how they did these things, because they are hardly aware of it. Partly because of this highly embodied style of interaction, participants potentially have a very vivid sense of being present in the virtual world, though this also depends on the emotions stimulated during their navigation of the space.

8.2.3 Designing for Emotion

Emotions that persist for more than a very short time are called moods. The most common conceptualization of mood defines it in terms of two dimensions, valence (degree of pleasantness) and arousal (Watson and Tellegen 1985; Russel et al. 1989). With this definition we can identify five different moods: high valence and high arousal (HVHA), high valence and low arousal (HVLA), low valence and low arousal (LVLA), low valence and high arousal (LVHA), and neutral (medium valence and medium arousal). See Figure n. Specific, more transient emotions can also be described by their valence and arousal properties. Morris (1995) provides valence and arousal scores for a number of emotion adjectives, such as carefree (HVLA) and terrified (LVHA).

Since upward movement suggests improving or lightening mood (HVLA), whereas downward movement corresponds to deteriorating or darkening mood (LVHA), we positioned Paradiso above Purgatorio (the everyday world) and this above Inferno (Hell). See Fig. 8.2. This rather obvious linking can be theoretically supported by, for example, the Experiential Realism of Lakoff and Johnson (1980, 1999), who point to the way we use phrases such "I'm feeling down", "He's really flying high", "She's under the weather", etc. These zones are also intended to evoke the emotions related to each mood.

Paradiso was designed so that the user will have an experience that reflects a relaxed, even transcendent state of mind—where things happen as if internally. Paradiso is located above the clouds, so the sun always shines. The sun remains fixed in one place. The view from Paradiso shows infinite sky above (and to the sides) and cloud layer below. As the visitor moves around Paradiso, he/she hears various heavenly sounds in different places. The sounds are modulated according to how high the visitor flies. In the sky, there are mandalas and castles in the background (see Fig. 8.3).

The visitor can sink down into the cloud, but only to neck level, i.e. the lowest viewpoint is the level of the top of the clouds. Collision detection prevents the visitor from going down through the clouds unless her breathing is shallow and irregular. When this happens, and if the visitor is in the designed place for it, he/she will sink down to inferno (the hellish zone). Boredom, or simple curiosity may lead to this, because Heaven is pleasant but rather boring. For this reason, one is unlikely to feel mentally present in Paradiso for long, even if apparently still located there.

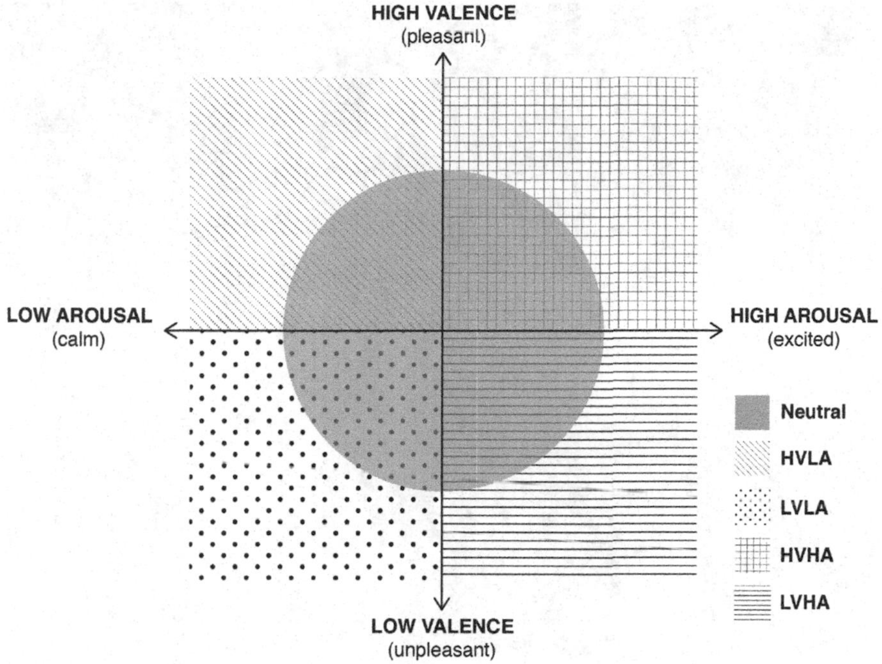

Fig. 8.2 Valence and arousal space divided into five mood states

The Inferno is an unpleasant place (see Fig. 8.4), with discordant sounds which we are designing, sudden loud noises in unpredictable places, perhaps screams, noises of machinery, low frequencies and explosions. Fog pervades the whole zone, with both distance- and particle-based elements. Ghosts, and other unpleasant-looking things, sometimes emerge out of the fog. The centre of the Inferno is a lively, large and noisy fire. Here there are also some of the most off-putting noises: screams, things smashing and breaking. It is unpleasant to be close to the fire. There are a few places that can take the visitor out of inferno. Depending on the place the visitor is transferred to Purgatorio or to Paradiso. To achieve this, the participant has to breathe deeply and calmly, and solve the puzzle of the maze, even though he/she is in an unpleasant, scary place. This is one way in which the environment stimulates self-knowledge and self-control.

Purgatorio represents the everyday world (Fig. 8.5). There are streets, a park and a beach, though there are no people. The participant can navigate around by leaning in different directions. As in the other zones, there are certain places where the participant may move to a different zone, in this case up to Paradiso, or down to Inferno.

Fig. 8.3 Image from Paradiso

We found that the three layers do indeed invoke different emotional responses. Using reported valence and arousal as indicators, Paradiso was judged to be relatively pleasant and calm (though boring), Inferno was unpleasant and stressful, and Purgatorio was more or less neutral (and fairly interesting). See Fig. 8.6.

8.2.4 Emptiness and Curiosity

The main goal of the Exploratorium was to stimulate curiosity, leading to exploration—both of the space and of the emotions generated in different parts of the space—and a consequent sense of control and empowerment. We chose to limit interaction to navigation. Participants cannot select or move objects in the space, only to move around as in a dream space. We emphasize exploration, and this starts from emptiness. Without movement, there is nothing to focus the attention on, nothing to be conscious of. Movement brings experiences which provoke curiosity, and so stimulate further self-motivated exploration—or resting in a part of the world the participant chooses, based on the emotions generated there.

Paradiso is pleasant and relaxing, but empty. The participant likes to be there, but is curious about something else. In Purgatorio, there is more to explore, but the world is bounded and empty of people. And Inferno is like a maze, dark and

Fig. 8.4 Inferno

forbidding, but very engaging. The participant has to enter the most unpleasant part, at the heart of the maze where horrible sights and sounds crowd in on him/her, and throw himself/herself into the fire of Hell to escape—all the while breathing calmly and deeply.

8.3 Morphogenetic Prototyping in Blended Reality Space

Design disciplines have always been interested in biological growth as a potent metaphor for design. By interpreting this metaphor as a process, it is possible to represent design artefacts as the result of a series of pseudo biological developmental stages (McGinley et al. 2018). Here, we describe an approach termed "*morphogenetic prototyping*" which aims to use these stages to support a multi-dimensional design process and *design experience* for the development of "morphogenetic prototypes" (McGinley et al. 2016).

Through this process, an axe was selected as the metaphor for the bricolage experience to relate the affordance of carving or sculpturing to the simulation of a pseudo biological subdivision. An axe prototype (Fig. 8.7) was used to identify appropriate gestures to map to biological behaviours in order to trigger the simulation of staged pseudo biological processes in the design model. The Bricolage as design

Fig. 8.5 Purgatorio

approach requires a new interface to support this experience. It is suggested that a metaphor defined as "carving or sculpturing" should be reinforced with *primitive interaction design.*

The use of an axe to carve (Schkolne et al. 2004) and a "carving" metaphor based on drawing (cutting) gestures in the morphogenetic prototyping process provides users with awareness, immersion, involvement, naturalness and realness (Hoshi and Waterworth 2009). The material, shape, size, texture and weight attributes of the axe provide an augmented improvement in a blended reality environment, and hence increase the sense of perceived presence in the blended reality space (Waterworth and Hoshi 2016). It is appropriate for carving to identify an appropriate user interface for primitive interaction.

8.3.1 Mapping Gestures for Blended Reality Space

Morphogenetic prototyping in blended reality space is a conceptual space where designers could draw parallels between artefact, biology and everyday life. The stone axe known as a Celt is one of the first tools used by mankind. It seemed fitting that this primitive tool evolves for the twenty-first century and be used as the first tangible user

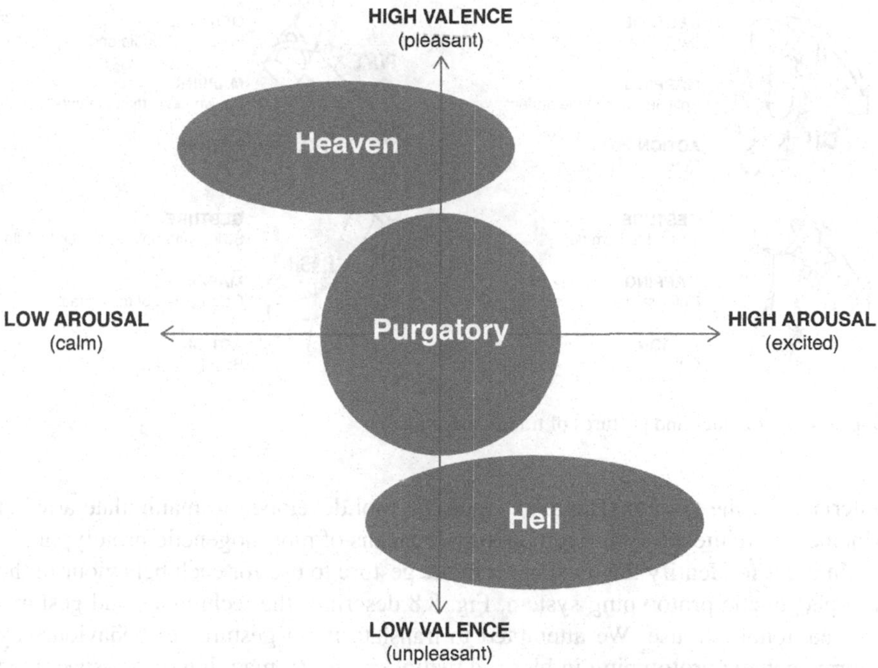

Fig. 8.6 Emotional experiences in the three zones of the Exploratorium

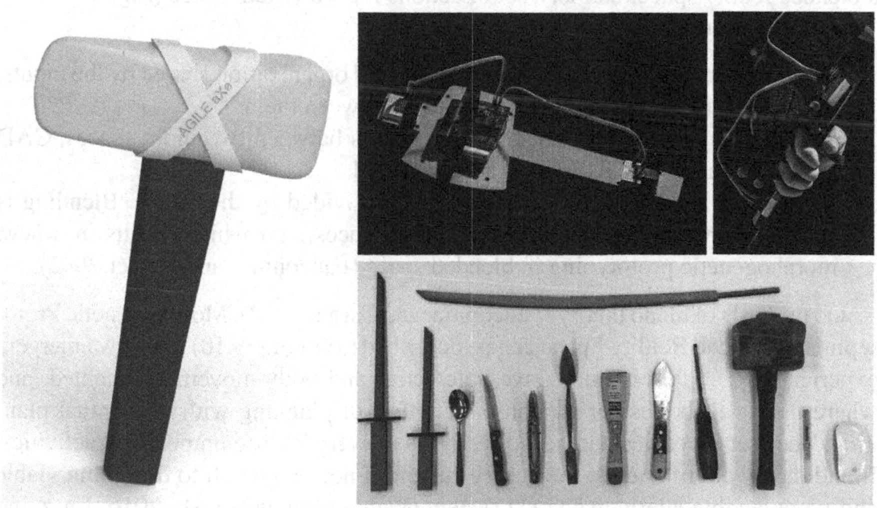

Fig. 8.7 The axe prototype interaction tool

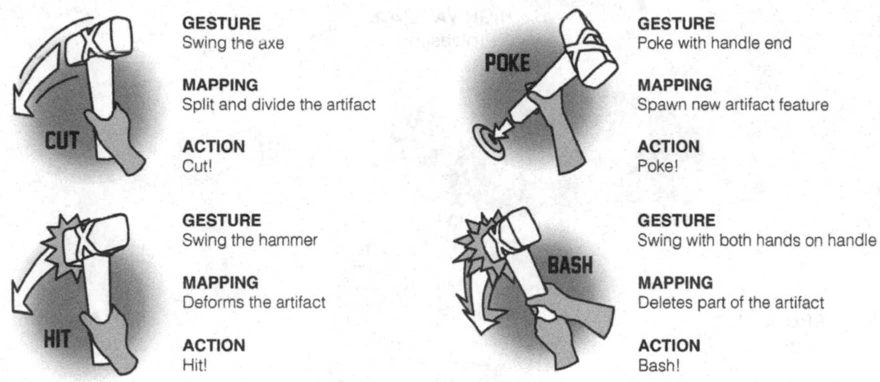

Fig. 8.8 Techniques and gestures of traditional axe use

interface for the system. The axe is a design tool developed to manipulate artefact (including architecture) through biology as means of morphogenetic prototyping.

In order to identify the most appropriate gesture to use for each behaviour in the morphogenetic prototyping system, Fig. 8.8 describes the techniques and gestures of traditional axe use. We attempted to translate these gestures to behaviours by morphogenetic prototyping in blended reality space. By mapping (cross-space) the gestures to meanings and functions within the scope of design and biology, we created a blended reality space, that is, a set of actions for the virtual space (Fig. 8.9).

Blending works as follows (see Fig. 8.10):

1. Generic space: It reflects abstract structure and organization shared by the inputs, and defines the core cross-space mapping between them.
2. Cross-space mapping: Elements and relations between two input spaces, CAD operation and physical carving, are connected.
3. Blend: It is a new emergent structure not provided by the inputs. Blending is an operation that is applied to two input spaces, and which results in a new, morphogenetic prototyping in blended space (Fauconnier and Turner 2002).

On the basis of blend theory (Fauconnier and Turner 2002), Morphogenetic Prototyping in Blended Reality Space can be described (as in Fig. 8.10) as a new emergent experience space that is immersive, interactive and body-movement oriented, and where there will be less or no conscious effort of planning with conceptual planning. The user perceives and acts directly, as in everyday life unmediated activities. Blend theory contributes to the establishment of new approach to designing viable and more flexible alternative CAD system (Waterworth and Hoshi 2016; Imaz and Benyon 2007).

The axe as a metaphor for carving in morphogenetic prototyping creates the first steps towards artificial life in the form of morphogenetically prototyped designs. As the next step, the physical movement of the axe has to be tracked by movement sensors to provide a primitive interaction to a morphogenetic prototyping design interface (Fig. 8.11).

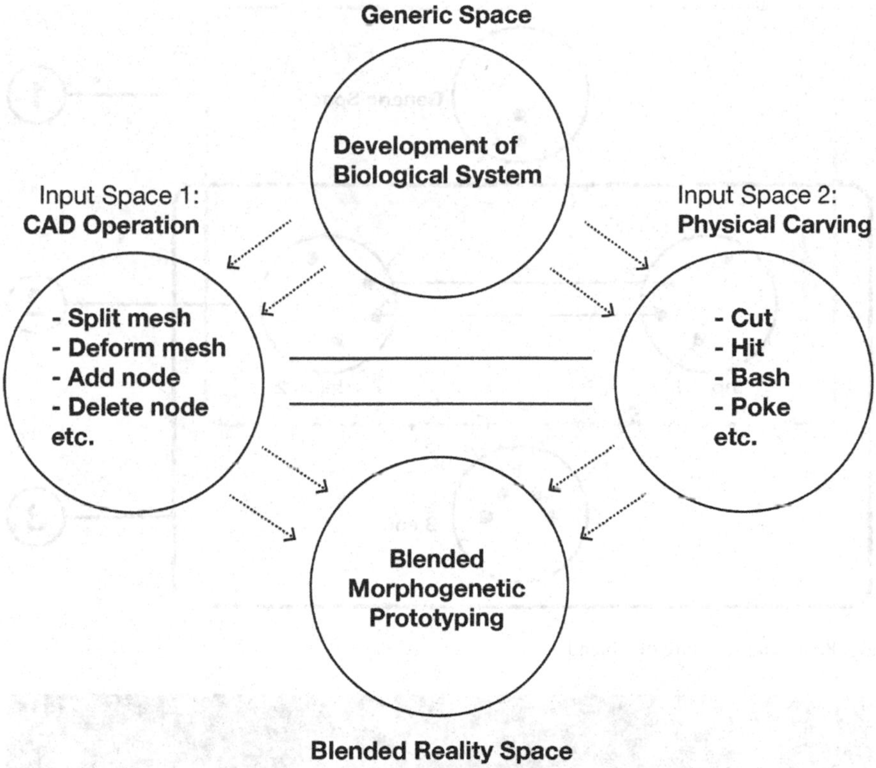

Fig. 8.9 Conceptual spaces for a blended morphogenic prototyping environment

8.3.2 System Configuration

A blended reality space was created in order to immerse the user within the field of design. This was done by setting up the Opti Track motion capture system then linking this to Unity, our chosen virtual reality program. An Oculus Rift headset and the Opti Track motion capture system were linked together to communicate in synchronization within Unity. A human avatar for Unity was downloaded, and the headset camera was adjusted in such a way that the viewpoint of the user in blended reality corresponded with their physical body.

An axe, which connects the digital with the physical space, was developed and modelled using 3D printing techniques. The axe encased movement sensors which was then linked to Unity. The user was able to cut the model in blended reality, splitting the mesh while holding the axe. The data from the manipulated model was sent back to Rhino/Grasshopper, and the results of the mutation were documented and analysed.

A dynamic 3D model was created using modelling software Rhino/Grasshopper. The data from the 3D model was then streamed to Unity in real time. The streamed

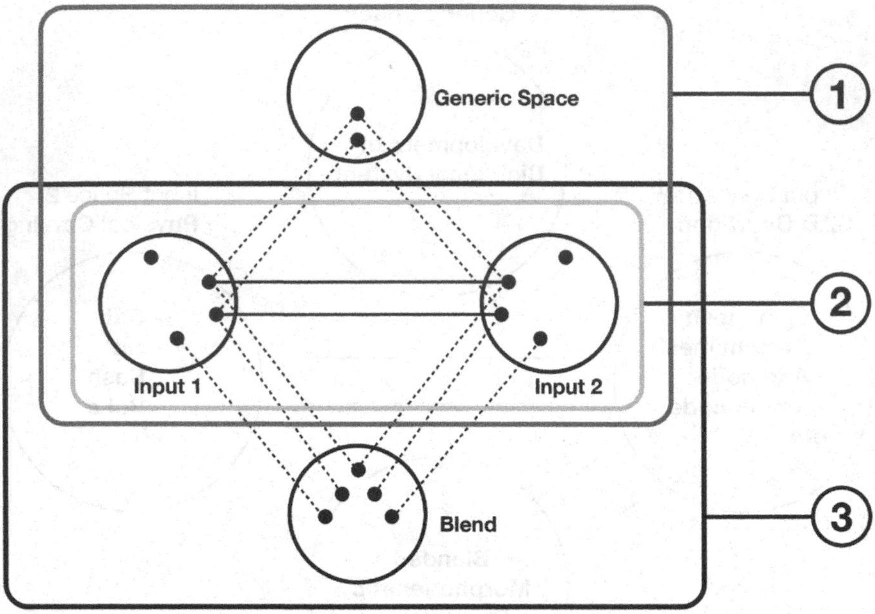

Fig. 8.10 The structure of a blend

Fig. 8.11 Movement tracking of axe actions

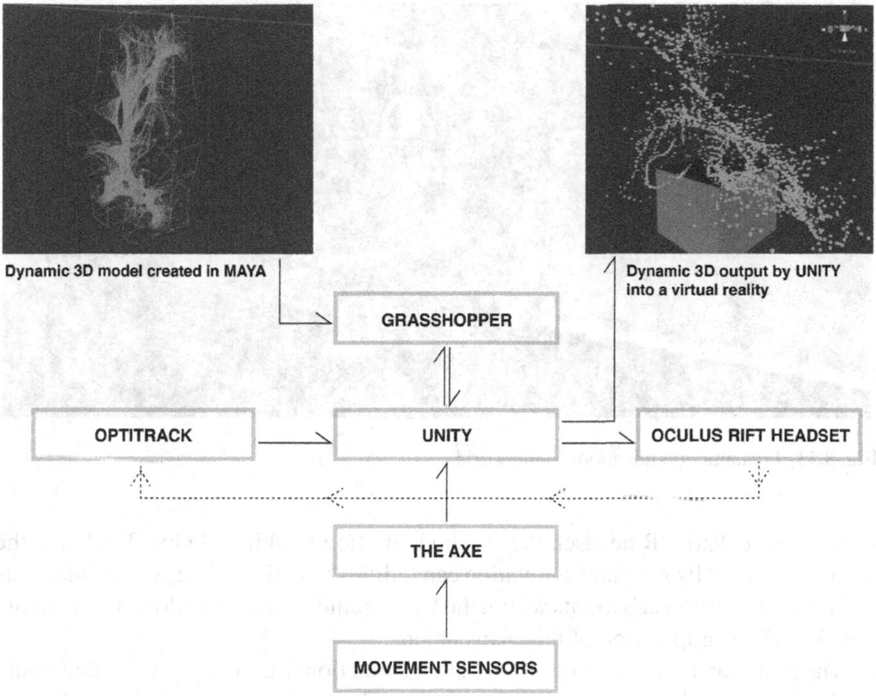

Fig. 8.12 Flow diagram of interaction scheme

data could be seen and manipulated by the user standing within the blended reality space. The manipulated data was also successfully sent back to the original modelling software as a new iteration of the original design. Using the axe and a carving motion, the user within the blended reality space, was able to manipulate and make changes to the model. The user feels the immediate feedback from their actions as their surrounding environment changes (Fig. 8.12).

8.3.3 Motion Tracking in Blended Reality Space

Through this project, the Design X team[2] explored methods to improve the quality and accuracy of the user's presence in a blended reality space. To achieve this, the team created an experimental system combining the head tracking capabilities

[2]The AgileX project was funded by the University of South Australia's Research Themes Investment Scheme. The AgileX project team (listed in random order): Tim McGinley, Brett Abroe, Linus Tan, Dianela Mitteberger, Tiziano Derme, Manuel Muehlbauer, Prof Simon Biggs, James Wilson, Daish Malani, Dr Kei Hoshi, Shane Haddy, Thomas Kuys, Gwilyn Saunders, Kelly Carpenter, Timothy Tuppence, Clare Timpani, Conor Mannering, William Mount, Andrew Lymn-Penning, Roxane Adams, Mark Langman, Fraser Murison.

Fig. 8.13 Dynamic modifications to the world

of the Oculus Rift VR headset, the full-body motion tracking of Opti Track and the modelling, visualization and simulation capabilities of Unity 5. The system interprets and articulates the user's inputs within the Unity game engine and allows the dynamic creation and manipulation of the environment.

The aim was to create a comfortable and functional user experience that could be developed to the point that the software or hardware do not inhibit the use of the virtual space. To achieve this, we developed a system between several software suites (Grasshopper, Rhino, 3DS Max, Maya, etc.) and pieces of hardware that can be modified in real time as the user makes changes to the game world (Fig. 8.13).

8.4 Discussion

Our first example illustrates several of the principles that we have discussed earlier in the book: the use of myth as inspiration, unconscious (embodied) interaction and designing for specific emotions. The main goal of the Exploratorium was to stimulate curiosity, leading to exploration—both of the space and of the emotions generated in different parts of the space—and a consequent sense of control and empowerment. The project precedes this book by many years, but it was one of the inspirations for the primitive interaction approach.

In the second example of primitive interaction design, we can imagine what would happen if primitive people played with such tools in virtual-physical blended space. The system focused on simple interaction between human and a tool in a virtual space. There was no conceptual plan from the beginning, but through play, we "explored" things that were tools which were made for specific purposes and means, and the environment in which we were placed was the total relationship of those tools. This process of discovering one's own thoughts is basically a bricolage-like activity. It becomes important to find the problem to be solved and to find the solution. Often discoveries are made among the things that are already there. There should be no prior concept of what the things were and what their purpose was.

Both examples are based on the insight that interactions should be designed as challenges to existing concepts of interaction. This opens up new understandings of what could be interactions and what interaction could be (for). By this view, interaction is not a given need filled up with functionalities. Ambiguity about interaction is what drives new forms of interaction. It involves the effective use of negative space which, through constraint and absence, encourages audiences to make complements, drawing on images from their own experiential knowledge.

References

Davies C (1998) Osmose: notes on being in immersive virtual space. In: Digital creativity, vol 9, No 2. Swets and Zeitlinger, London, ISSN 0957–9133

Fauconnier G, Turner M (2002) The way we think: conceptual blending and the mind's hidden complexities. Basic Books

Hoshi K, Waterworth J (2009) Tangible presence in blended reality space. Presented at the PRESENCE 2009, pp 1–10

Imaz M, Benyon D (2007) Designing with blends. MIT Press, London, England

Ishii H (2008) Tangible bits: beyond pixels. In: Proceedings of the 2nd international conference on Tangible and embedded interaction (pp. 15–25).

Lakoff G (1999) Philosophy in the flesh: the embodied mind and its challenge to western thought. Basic Books

Lakoff G, Johnson M (1980) Metaphors we live by. University of Chicago Press, Chicago

McGinley T, Hoshi K, Iacopetta L (2015) MorphoCarve: carving morphogenetic prototypes. In: Presented at the 6th conference of the international association of societies of design research, Brisbane, Australia

McGinley T, Hoshi K, Gruber P, Haddy S, Zavoleas Y, Tan L, Blaiklock D (2018) A Katana design experience. In: Intersections in simulation and gaming. Springer, Cham, pp. 134–148

McGinley T, Hoshi K, Haddy S (2016) Carving morphogenetic prototypes with a Katana

Morris JD (1995) Observations: SAM: the self-assessment Manikin. An efficient cross-cultural measurement of emotional response. J Advertising Res 35(6): 63–68

Russell JA, Weiss A, Mendelsohn GA (1989) Affect grid: a single-item scale of pleasure and arousal. J Personality Soc Psych. 57:493–502

Schkolne S, Ishii H, Schroder P (2004) Immersive design of DNA molecules with a tangible interface. In: IEEE Visualization 2004, pp. 227–234

Waterworth JA, Hoshi K (2016) Human-experiential design of presence in everyday blended reality

Watson D, Tellegen A (1985) Toward a consensual structure of mood. Psychol Bull 98:219–235

Chapter 9
Towards a New Culture of Interaction Design

The sound of the freezing of snow over the land seemed to roar deep into the earth. There was no moon. The stars, almost too many of them to be true, came forward so brightly that it was as if they were falling with the swiftness of the void.
Kawabata, Yasunari (1996). Snow country. Trans. Edward G. Seidensticker. New York: Vintage.

Abstract Design is seen in this book not merely as making technology easier to use, aesthetically attractive or economically consumable and profitable, but as opening up new possibilities, creative perspectives leading to new ways of interacting and being with technology. Design may have limited power, in itself, to change the world, but it can also be a critical tool to monitor the implications of new developments appearing on the market through progress in science and technology. For this, we must have possibility to change our beliefs, behaviours and attitudes within a new culture of interaction design.

9.1 Where Have We Been?

In this book, we have built on some of the ideas introduced in our earlier book "Human-Experiential Design of Presence in Everyday Blended Reality: Living in the Here and Now" (Waterworth and Hoshi 2016). We set out to explore what we call primitive interaction design, to release designers from the spell they are under and, through them, the people who buy the products. A consideration of the spiritual dimension, and of myth, of emptiness and of the unconscious should come as a revelation to the profession and inspire new ways that design can make technology more meaningful and relevant to our lives, embodying primitive elements of human experience and understanding. This potentially opens up design to everyone and grounds interaction designers more in the human experience of being.

Interaction design has, for several decades, sought to aim for the—as yet unrealized—ideal of seamless integration of hardware/software, while taking account of human experience, the environment, and interaction, and learning from them. This

© Springer Nature Switzerland AG 2020

K. Hoshi and J. Waterworth, *Primitive Interaction Design*,
Human–Computer Interaction Series,
https://doi.org/10.1007/978-3-030-42954-6_9

ideal includes the idea of using Internet-enabled and other digital devices with little or no conscious effort. But conventional design thinking and methods mean that this goal cannot be achieved.

Design is thought to inspire and impress people's awareness, but when things or systems are used in a natural flow, people become unaware of those things and do not consider themselves as "users" of them. Designed things disappear from perception and people subconsciously try to harmonize with their environment. When walking on a crowded pedestrian crosswalk, people are unaware of the shoes or socks they are wearing and are not consciously thinking about the ground they are walking on. On a busy crosswalk, pedestrians walk without colliding with each other. "Ma" is subconsciously perceived and each route is created there. "Ma" blends into subconscious acts. People are constantly and subconsciously seeking opportunities to maintain balance with things, systems, the environment and nature. It is also creative. People are creative by nature.

From now on, the search for "ma" must be included as well. "ma" is not a position to negate or confront science, but rather aims to inherit scientific exploration and encourage new creations. The current limitations of science to entities and their associations should be replaced, and a more liberal universality should be sought. In the process of pursuing the objective facts of entities and their associations, science has called for abandoning the concepts of self and ordinariness while becoming the third party in order to know the essence of an entity or association. The quest for "ma" aims to revive the concepts of self and ordinariness and take a more subjective approach. Taking advantage of self and ordinariness must be much more universal.

Genuine design is entropy that aims to deconstruct order. However, entropy is unable to continue to survive alone. Rather, it fulfils a role as an activator for the mere shell of order that is present within the dynamics of the structure. Design faces the chaos of the "periphery" and confronts its own rebirth as an intermediary between the "centre" and the margins.

Primitive interaction design is based on providing "ma" and foregoing awareness of things that exist in the flow. The "ma" in design is what is created subconsciously which exists during the process of dynamic interaction between people and their environment, where we extract information from our accumulated physical experience, classify it and bring it back into our body.

We have argued that while the vitality and polysemy of the "periphery" ideally serve as a driving force to activate the border of the centre, design has become a tool to serve system science, engineering and business. As such, the vitality of genuine design is lost. Design should serve as a challenger that reinvigorates the "centre" through its vitality and ability to provoke. In order to be perceived as an invigorate society in itself, design must be sufficiently provocative in the periphery, and the designer must be able to actively go back and forth through the mechanism of the connection point between the "centre" and the "periphery". Vitality and polysemy decline if the regularity, averageness and normality of the "centre" continue uninterrupted. The vitality of culture is ensured through the conflict between the "centre" and concepts divorced from the cultural context such as *infantile play, the heterogeneous, the latent/unconscious and emptiness*. Provocativeness is only achieved through being different.

As a study of the mind and body, Buddhism philosophy speaks to highly relevant topics, including consciousness, mind/body and self/other. Disciplines in science, philosophy, engineering and design need to work together to ensure that human beings will derive a benefit from the rapid growth of technology. Science has so far explored only the physical "entity". Paradoxically, technological changes exploiting the progress of science have made our lives more "primitive", in the sense in which the word was once applied in a disparaging way to the cultures of indigent societies.

We have not aimed to highlight conflict between the East and West, nor for any categorization. There is no tangible boundary between the East and West. The discussions which seem as if there were a confrontation between them are solely for the purpose of offering a glimpse of what design could be like in the future. We have not suggested which is superior, but rather explored future design possibilities by making the most of the philosophical differences between the East and West.

At the heart of design lies a question with no right answers—"What is design?" Unable to provide a clear and concrete answer to the question, we have discussed the practical position of design in relation to business, engineering and social science, and offered new directions for design to take. In this final chapter, we review our progress and position. To do that, we need to start by considering the present in relation to trends for the future.

9.2 Where Are We Going?

There are two directions in progressing interaction design: to "Make design come true" and to "Understand what design is". The latter, concerning the nature of design, is philosophically difficult. As its nature is unclear, design may go around and around engineering, business and art and end up being their servant. In the field of design research, which is more academic and intellectual than the design scene itself, once one (the self in general) interprets the world of design as he/she likes, he/she then stores the interpretation structure. He/she often tries to understand design within his/her interpretation by rejecting any other design outside the framework of his/her interpretation, ending up with no escape. If we modify the net to capture the world, we should be able to grow the stored knowledge freely. However, as is often the case with researchers, they would capture and restrain themselves within a tiny yet cumbersome net, ending up being fixed within a narrow and limited point of view. Getting out of it seems very hard. Because they have become the core in relation to the rim. They need to blend themselves with the rim in order to get out of there. Eastern thought and this book may act as a guide. We would be happy if design in the muddy mainstream were liberated into a clear stream and if many designers felt the new flow of design without being aware of it.

The science called design, especially the field of human-centred interaction design, has been attempting to produce design as a template for human intelligence, as in embedded AI features or a robot. Artefacts designed according to the Eastern perspective should be regarded as a part of the world from the beginning. The East can help to find a way towards a completely contrasting direction. Design should be made by making the best of all the Western and Eastern wisdom that have been piled up by our ancestors for a long time. To foster such a process is one of the aims of this book.

Increasingly, interaction design is the design of the interface between artificially made intelligence and our everyday life. With Artificial Intelligence evolving day by day, companies can offer new features and services as part of their business. AI is penetrating our everyday life as a technology which brings convenience. It is difficult to grasp what design is, but without doubt, AI is at the heart of the intersection.

For example, AI objectifies what facial expressions represent. However, the harder AI tries to project what lies in the depth of the human mind, the more difficult this pursuit becomes. As AI objectifies invisible intelligence, it gets farther away from intelligence. It is similar to how the harder we try to define design in words, the more remote design becomes. What is definable is predictable. However, no one can possibly predict design objectively, nor is the objective prediction the essential goal intended for design.

We, human beings and all sentient creatures, have profound minds and intelligence inside ourselves. We generate the world that contains us. Sadly, artefacts today do not seem to give us profound resonance when we try to have a dialogue or interaction with them.

Designed artefacts will increasingly have intelligence and penetrate the human world more and more. They have the potential to change human communication, society and the world. This intelligence may be able to contribute to the stability of human beings by understanding people. However, the first step must be taken by us to understand humanity, regardless of West or East. The act of design will give us opportunities to understand humanity, whether its object is a doorknob or AI, and play a role in the reintegration of science and society. Design is one fruit of human wisdom; at the same time, it has a potential for improving the world. If we can liberate ourselves from the restrictions that surrounds us, design will become the subject of transformation. This is the philosophy of Primitive Interaction Design.

9.3 Concluding Comments

Design is seen in this book not merely as making technology easier to use, aesthetically attractive or economically consumable and profitable, but as opening up new possibilities, creative perspectives leading to new ways of interacting and being with technology. Design may have limited power, in itself, to change the world, but it can also be a critical tool to monitor the implications of new developments appearing on the market through progress in science and technology. For this, we must have the possibility to change our beliefs, behaviours and attitudes within a new culture of interaction design.

Our approach monitors and refocuses mainstream design rather than seeking to replace it, and questions prevailing values and their underlying assumptions through design activities in the real world. As well as presenting an alternative view of design, we hope that this will help people become more discerning consumers, encouraging them to demand more from industry and society as perspicacious consumers. The book does not aim to position design or designers on the moral high ground or as social saviours. On the contrary, we have conveyed a different, two-part message. First, by returning to primitives—of design, of meaning, of existence—we are making designers more human; and second, by exploring primitive design techniques we provide tools for all humans to be designers.

Society has become more savage and less cultured, despite—or because of—the interactive devices that permeate our lives. In this book, we have tried to shed light on how our thinking of design and information-based society should adapt to this by using more universal thinking and aspects of human consciousness/unconsciousness in a new, "primitive" coexistence with modern information technology. We believe that this view of design is more enlightened and humane, and has the potential to raise awareness of the consequences of our actions in our current information society.

Reference

Waterworth J, Hoshi K (2016) Human-experiential design of presence in everyday blended reality: living in the here and now. Springer, Switzerland

Printed in the United States
by Baker & Taylor Publisher Services

Printed in the United States
by Baker & Taylor Publisher Services